MW00827217

UNTWISTING TWISTED TRUTH

LOVING JESUS MORE THAN MY HOMOSEXUAL LIFE

Marilyn K. Snyder

www.HealedHeart.net
Marilyn@HealedHeart.net

TRILOGY CHRISTIAN PUBLISHERS

Tustin, CA

Trilogy Christian Publishers

A Wholly Owned Subsidiary of Trinity Broadcasting Network

2442 Michelle Drive

Tustin, CA 92780

Untwisting Twisted Truth

Rights Department, 2442 Michelle Drive, Tustin, CA 92780.

Trilogy Christian Publishing/TBN and colophon are trademarks of Trinity Broadcasting Network.

Cover design by Jeff Summers

Author photo credit: Christina Graves

For information about special discounts for bulk purchases, please contact Trilogy Christian Publishing.

Trilogy Disclaimer: The views and content expressed in this book are those of the author and may not necessarily reflect the views and doctrine of Trilogy Christian Publishing or the Trinity Broadcasting Network.

Manufactured in the United States of America

10 9 8 7 6 5 4 3 2 1

Library of Congress Cataloging-in-Publication Data is available.

ISBN: 979-8-88738-826-7

E-ISBN: 979-8-88738-827-4 (ebook)

Fondly dedicated to:
Those who loved me just like Jesus...

~ Miss Ruthie Bailey ~
Thank you for taking me under your wing to love me,
to mentor me, and to train me in ministry.
God used you to breathe life into my wounded soul.
Thank you for believing in me!

~ Pastor Jonathan ~
Your gentle and loving spirit reflected Christ
and launched my healing toward wholeness.
I would not be where I am today if you had not loved me like Jesus!
Thank you for encouraging me in the completion of this book.

~ Pastor Andy ~
You gave me a second chance at friendship
and showed me how to forgive.
Your example of Christ ministering to broken people gave me hope!
Thank you for letting me join in your basketball games.

~ Mark and Emily Dorman ~
You taught me much about life and unconditional love.
Thank you for opening your home
and your lives to be my healing balm.
Thank you for trusting me!

Acknowledgments

To my Lord and Savior: King Jesus—You are the reason any of this is possible! I am so overwhelmed at Your gracious love toward me! Thank You for pursuing me and for guiding me through this journey. May You receive all the glory!

To my children: Micah Snyder and Matthew Snyder—what amazing gifts you are to me! You guys have been so patient with this writing process. Thank you for your encouragement to press on in this project! Your endless support and challenges for me to keep it real have greatly benefited the final outcome of this undertaking. Thanks for sharing this writing adventure with me. Love you to the moon and back! You're the best!

To my parents: (the late) Victor and Shirley Weberg—thank you for the legacy of your faith, for standing firm on the truth of God's Word and not wavering. Thank you, Dad, for supporting me and sharing some bubbly grape juice with me the last time we were together, celebrating as you "counted it all joy" for the prize that awaited you on the other side. Thank you, Mom, for suggesting I contact TBN for publication just a couple of days before you crossed into glory. That was your stamp of approval as well as God's guidance for the next step. I am so indebted to you both for all your prayers! We'll see you on the other side!

To my siblings and their spouses: Brad and Diane Weberg, Roland and Kate Weberg, Cheryl and Jeff Lee, Karyn and Kevin O'Shea, and Karyl (and the late Tom) Ross—thank you for loving me and your gift of forgiveness, which inspired me on toward healing. You all mean the world to me! Karyn, your encouragement to write over and over and over again is part of the reason this is done!

To my copy editor: Dr. Barbara Sherman—you've been my biggest cheerleader, my sounding board, my editor, my lunch-time mentor, my prayer warrior! Thank you for being willing to meet with an inexperienced writer and give your time, your insight, and, most importantly, your friendship! Thanks for believing in me!

To my developmental editor: Alyssa Smith—your early editing work on this project was so essential. Thank you for asking hard questions that had to be answered for things to make sense. Thank you for stretching me and making me express in words more than I ever thought I could. So appreciative of you!

To my encouragers/prayers/beta readers/supporters: Sharon Becker, Michelle Bowers, Kathie and Derrick Canipe, Karen Collins, Yolanda and Mike Devillers, Angela Dudley, Val Garcia, Randy Griffin, Mary Hensley, Rodney Jackson, Kay Lain, Susan Muhoro, Martha Ordonez, Karyn O'Shea, Buck Romero, Nedra Rose, Mark Stillwell, Diane Weberg, several Bible study and small groups—you'll never know what a great impact your gifts, time, energy, prayers, and honest feedback had until we reach heaven. So incredibly grateful for each one of you and many others who prayed for me and this project!

To my childhood friend: Sharon Becker—your gift of welcoming me is forever etched on my heart. Thank you for not giving up on me and for being my friend for many, many years!

To my coffee-drinking buddies: Debbie Rhodes and Pat Johnston—I'm amazed at all God taught me through your friendships. Thanks for all the mall memories. We may start that coffee ministry yet!

To TBN and the publishing team—so thankful to be partnering with you in ministry. I cannot wait to see what God does with this!

Disclaimer: some names and places have been changed to protect those who are also forgiven and have received God's grace.

Contents

CONTENTS

Author's Note

I write about "marriage" to my transsexual partner and Kris being called "he" even after I left the relationship. This is what I believed to be true at the time. My beliefs for marriage are clearly stated in my statement of faith in appendix D. When I walked away from homosexuality, I had not yet processed the whole idea of identity, and the pronoun issue took some time for me to work through. I believe she was made a female in God's image. I left this in the book to show that it may take some time for someone walking out of this lifestyle to develop a godly viewpoint.

Marching Orders

Virginia
2016

Fall was in the air. In the cool of the morning, I sat on my porch swing, soaking it all in: the gently falling leaves, the deer quietly making their way through the yard, the beauty of stillness before the day's demands. My prayers were thankful that day. Life was fairly calm as I enjoyed the quiet time. That was when I heard it.

"And Lord, thank You for..."

"It is time to tell your story."

"Wait—what God? For a minute there, I thought You said to tell my story. That is not what You said, was it? I mean, You couldn't really be serious."

"Yes, it is time. People need to hear."

"You do remember it was more than three decades ago, don't You? Isn't that information a bit old to be sharing now? I have met so many people since then who would be shocked, maybe even angry, that I wasn't 'real' with them. I mean, what would they think?"

"Marilyn, this is not about you and your reputation but about Me and My grace. It is about what I did in your life and what I want to do in others' lives as well. It is time."

"But, God, don't You think we have missed the prime opportunity? Everything has drifted so far from what You designed. Isn't it a little late?"

"While you were married, you were not allowed to share this story of My grace in your life. Now you can. Let Me take care of the timing. You just start writing—I will handle the rest. You have already learned that obedience is hard sometimes. Will you trust Me and obey Me once again?"

"Yes, Lord. Yes!"

~ ~ ~ ~ ~

This is not the type of book one dreams of writing, but sometimes life takes the broken road, and you gain experience and knowledge you were never looking for. Life circumstances, coupled with decisions I would change if I could, gave me a story about homosexuality coming face to face with God's unconditional love and amazing grace. I am not an expert in all things LGBTQ, but I know not everyone who finds themselves in that lifestyle has complete peace and wants to be there.

My prayer is that, by taking you on my journey, you might see the LGBTQ through Jesus' eyes. May we all be challenged to immerse ourselves in an intimate relationship with Jesus, spiking the curiosity of those who watch, giving them a desire to have a friendship with Jesus like ours, and ultimately, drawing them to His heart.

To the parent/family member of an LGBTQ: You are not alone. Jesus is captivated by your precious one more than you are. He wants to walk alongside you, helping you learn to see and love as He does.

To the body of Christ: We are called to be a conduit of His boundless compassion. May we seek out ways to be Jesus' hands and feet to people, loving the LGBTQ just as Jesus loved us, without compromising the truth of God's Word.

Jesus loves you deeply right where you are!

To the LGBTQ who is curious about why I would walk away from homosexuality or wondering if anyone understands or cares about your thoughts and concerns: I care, and more importantly, Jesus cares! He sees you. He knows you. Your life matters to Him. Jesus loves you deeply right where you are!

MY JOURNEY INTO HOMOSEXUALITY

CHAPTER 1

Deceit's Death Grip

My Early Twenties
Colorado
1986

Deceit clung to me as my closest companion for several years. The initial, innocent grasp on my heart slowly tightened over time until, finally, its death grip held me firmly with no way to shake it off and break free. Today, however, I was on a quest to find a way to dump this persistent friend. My mind wavered between confusion and clarity about what I was sure to be truth. Or was it? There was not much of which I was absolutely sure. The battle raged inside until I was fully convinced black was white, and you could not have made me believe any differently. As time went on, I began to settle in to this new way of thinking. All I once knew to be wrong was now right. There was no changing my mind...yet.

A prayer conference at my church had sparked some uneasiness and doubt, digging up questions in my mind I thought I had buried for good. I was in the habit of holding everyone at bay, so finding someone I could trust enough to discuss my uncertainty with was rather difficult. How would I know if that person was telling the truth? Besides, if I finally figured out what truth was, how could I even begin to repair the damage that had been done? Was it worth trying? Where would I go from here?

Breathe!

Wandering the hallway back and forth between our offices was beginning to look slightly suspicious. I had decided I might be able to trust Ruthie. She appeared very motherly and as though she had gone through a lot of life experiences. Something about her gave the impression of safety.

Finally working up enough nerve, I stopped by her office and asked if we could talk at her home after work. Actually, I really needed to leave right away because I felt like I was going to be sick. We had worked on many projects together, and her home had become a second home to me. Something inside me sensed it would be the perfect place to dump my guts. What would happen after that was anybody's guess, but at least everything would be out in the open.

Out in the open! That thought scared me more than I could even admit. Living with the lies that I told others and myself had become so normal. I didn't know any other way. The volcano inside bubbled and churned, reaching a boiling point I could no longer control. I was about to erupt, so I knew I had better choose my audience, or things could get ugly.

As I walked into the small duplex, the familiar smell of Ruthie's southern cooking from the crock pot welcomed me.

Like coming home. Something about her place felt like a refuge. The perfect retreat where I could get lost in time. It was simple yet cozy. All sorts of books, framed memorable quotes, and seasoned knickknacks were scattered throughout. The orange and gold sectional from the 1970s was not the prettiest, but it definitely was the most comfortable sofa in the world. Her home was a place where I could normally kick back and relax— but not today.

Soft lighting lit the other side of the room as I settled into my spot on the sofa. I did not want her to see my face when we talked. Something was about to change, but I did not know exactly what my fate would be. I had become very good at deceiving myself, so I could live the lie and make it believable to those I came in contact with. Yet there was a fear of being found out. What if she already knew? What if she found out and hated me? What if I lost my job? What if I lost everything?

Breathe!

Crumbling inside, I could no longer hold the fragments of my life together. My mind was about to explode from the pressure. *If I leave now, she will never know I was here. Why don't I just tell her I changed my mind? What should I do?* If I left, would I ever have the nerve to come back again?

Breathe!

No more running. No more hiding. No more stories. I had to come clean and tell someone. Trust had become such a difficult (more like impossible) thing to do. Yet, I had to take the risk. I could not go on living like this—trying to make the lie acceptable and real was killing me.

As I waited, my mind drifted back to my childhood and the events that led up to this point. How on earth did I get here? What was it that caused me to fall for this trap? How could I get out of this deep, dark pit? Would I ever see my family again? Would I ever have a family of my own? What was the truth? Could anyone show me what truth was? Who could I believe?

Breathe!

Just breathe!

CHAPTER 2

Trust Betrayed

Childhood to Junior High
Minnesota
1960s-1970s

It was not exactly Mayberry, but the small farming community in the Upper Midwest where we lived was home. The town was comprised of about 300 people. The railroad and grain elevator were what kept the little place afloat. A few small businesses, the bank, a liquor store, three quaint churches, and a couple of gas stations lined the main street. There were no stoplights because, well, there just wasn't the need. It was the type of place where the biggest news in our four-page newspaper was publishing who had gone to someone's home for dinner, "and a good time was had by all."

Working in the fields, in the yard, and in the home was a way of life. My five older siblings were the ones who carried the majority of the workload. They were several years older than me, so it seemed like two separate families. By the time they all graduated, life on the farm looked much different than it had a few years earlier. Money was more available with one child at home instead of six. We ate out more and vacationed every year. Discipline was not necessary with a solitary compliant child, and curfews were a thing of the past. Hearing my siblings talk of memories is like listening to another family's story. It was as though I was an only child living in a home that held the memories of many.

Since there were numerous years between us, there was not a lot of camaraderie or shared entertainment. I was pretty much the annoying little sister who could not find anything to do and, should I stumble upon something exciting, had no one to do it with me. I am told I was good at doing what others instructed me to do. Calling me naive would be putting it mildly, but then, that should have been a blessing in my childhood.

My preschool friends were kids I knew from Sunday school. Our church was a half hour away, so my social life consisted of an hour a week—but I loved it! At our family's Sunday noon meal, I would ask if we could please go to church again at night for the evening service—only to be kicked by one of my teenage siblings, who was obviously not as interested. I quickly learned to keep my mouth shut about going back to church and cultivated an endurance for the long evenings with Casey Kasem's *American Top 40* playing quietly upstairs so no one downstairs would hear.

Despite any differing opinions, in my eyes, my siblings were the best! Although I do not remember much about the time they lived at home, some memories are cemented firmly in my mind:

- sitting on my brother's lap in the front seat of our packed red station wagon pointing out cows and horses on the way to church,
- being trapped in the house for days during snowstorms, wandering from one person to the next trying to pass the time, and getting so cold that I would crawl in bed just to warm up,
- snowstorms where the power went out and I would sit on their laps wrapped in a blanket, watching by the light of kerosene lanterns while the big people played Rook (our Christian alternative to regular playing cards), and
- my sisters stirring the chocolate syrup and peanuts into my vanilla ice cream and reading to me at bedtime.

They had the coolest things in their bedrooms. Being careful not to touch any of it, I was mesmerized for hours by:

- the pop-tab chain, which zigzagged several times across a bedroom ceiling,
- the gum wrapper chain that was nearly ten miles long—I was sure—and
- the little dresser that held amazing treasures, complete with marbles, unique rocks, and a petrified potato chip.

My all-time favorite birthday presents were getting things from their rooms they no longer wanted.

My parents both came from farming families, so this life was not new to them: careful planning, preparing the soil, sowing, trusting, waiting, and lots of prayer for the harvest. It was a tight ship of little spending with plenty of hard work. That was how they became successful.

They also planted within me some deep-rooted family memories. Dad loved to play tricks on my siblings, leaving empty pop cans balancing atop a half-opened door or piles of shoes in their darkened pathway. These and other traps would hinder any attempt for a quiet entrance late at night. His poetry, various bird calls, and drawings showed his creative style. The woodwork and carvings he designed and produced were absolute treasures. Mom's creativity was demonstrated through her crafts and sewing. Whether wall hangings, beautiful cross-stitch, or handmade Christmas decorations, there were often signs of a project in the works that would spice up and bring warmth to the home. Once in a while, we would gather around and sing the old hymns as she played the piano. Hearing "Because He Lives," "Great Is Thy Faithfulness," and other songs rich in faith takes me back to those precious memories.

One set of grandparents lived close by, and we would visit them regularly. Most of the time, I sat quietly in their living room and listened to the adults talk. But some Sundays, a couple of cousins would come, and we would play board games in the other room very quietly so we would not disturb anyone. There were only four cousins close to my age, and meeting up with them at my grandparents' home was a real treat. The other set of grandparents lived in Minneapolis. Visiting them meant more Rook and lots of laughter; although being so young, I was usually a spectator. The memories are rich with a sense of family on both sides; however, I did not always feel like I quite fit in with the "older reindeer games."

The school in town was one big building where kindergarten through twelfth grade attended all together. Part of it was the original building with worn steps, students' initials carved into wooden window frames, and aged walls that could tell some outrageous stories, given the chance. Additional sections had been adjoined for offices and the elementary students.

My parents, siblings, and older extended family had all attended the same school. When it came to my turn to go to elementary school, I loved it. Finally, I had something to do and people to do it with. Walking the halls to the gym or library and seeing my older siblings was my favorite event of the day. I looked forward to changing classes just like them someday.

Learning came easy for me. Most of all, I enjoyed the social aspect of school, wanting to be friends with everyone and not wanting anyone to feel left out. I would have fun with the popular kids at times and then go eat lunch or play at recess with those who were a little different and sometimes cast aside. Most of the time, I did not care which group it was as long as there was someone to play with. I always reached out to the new kids. If there happened to be a family relocating to the area, they usually moved away again after a year or two. There was not much keeping new families in that little town. I longed for the excitement the other kids must be having by moving to another place. But for now, my adventure would be in getting to know them and being their friend, regardless of how short their stay.

My first nephew arrived when I was six years old, and several other nieces and nephews followed close behind. Having family come home to visit was such a big deal to me because I would finally have someone to play with and a place where I fit. I became the resident babysitter and was pretty good at taking care of my nieces and nephews. Each time they left, I would count the days until another holiday or when one of them would be coming back for a visit. As the time for their arrival drew near, I would sit upstairs, lingering by an open window. Listening carefully as each car approached, I waited for one that sounded like it was slowing down. Finally, they would arrive, and I would race down the stairs when their vehicle turned into our driveway. I adored family and could not get enough of our time together. Most of the time, I enjoyed hanging out with the little people while my parents and siblings talked.

~ ~ ~ ~ ~

There was not much transition into junior high; after all, I had been in the same school for the last seven years since kindergarten. I did have to learn how to change classes, but that was more social time for me. A good kid with good manners and good grades—I thought those years would be a breeze. Little did I know the pain they would bring.

I continued to put forth effort into reaching out to others. The groups I seemed to fit into changed with each sport season. I had friends, but I did not seem to connect well with them outside of school. There was little in common unless we were involved in sports or music. At the time, we had a shared party telephone line, so I was only allowed to talk to friends for about five minutes before having to hang up. I did not like feeling isolated, as time seemed to move at a snail's pace when we were between sports or waiting for an upcoming music concert.

We changed churches prior to my seventh-grade year, and although I was nervous about being new, there was hope for fresh friendships. That church was also a half hour away in a different town. When we began visiting, the pastor's daughter and a couple of other girls would consistently ask if I would like to sit with them. They welcomed me just like I was doing for the students who relocated to my school. I soon joined the youth group's singing and drama ministry, which performed at other churches several times during the school year. I loved it! I loved getting to know other Christian kids. I loved older guys showing interest in me. I loved sitting together in church and being a part of a group. I finally fit in and found a place to belong!

The pastor's daughter, Sharon, and I became good friends. I would spend many Sundays at their home in between the morning and evening church services. I was learning so much about the Bible and what it meant to be a Christian. Sharon and I would talk and talk for hours—something I was so hungry for.

One thing I learned from Sharon was the importance of not only marrying someone with whom I had common Christian values but preparing early by dating someone who shared them as well. One Sunday, while we talked, we made a pact together to never date a non-Christian. This was something unfamiliar for me, having never discussed anything quite this personal with my family. It was fun having a special friend at church.

Since I was in this environment at church where I was sure all the guys were believers and very good, moral boys, I had no concern of spending time with any of them. Jack, in particular, seemed to have a special interest in me. He was several years older, which I thought was really cool. He was so sweet and began saving me a seat in church. He did not talk to me much, which was fine with me since I was shy about talking to boys, and having a crush on one was an unfamiliar experience.

Winter can get pretty cold in the Upper Midwest—even inside. I did not think anything was wrong when Jack offered his big winter jacket to cover our laps—until he began touching me inappropriately. I froze. "Was that what I thought it was?" I wondered. "Surely not." Beginning to question my judgment, I thought I must be imagining things. I did not know how to stand up for myself or when to tell people, "No!" Confident he really liked me, I continued sitting with him.

One night on the way home from one of our concerts, I was molested by him in the back of the bus—forced to have oral sex. Gaging and unable to breathe, he finally released his tight grip on my neck, so I was able to sit up. After catching my breath, I quickly moved to the front of the bus to ride the rest of the way home. Surrounded by friends and youth leaders, I said absolutely nothing.

I kept quiet. I did not understand what had happened to me. I was scared. I was confused. I was embarrassed. I felt dirty. Over the next couple of weeks, my body felt different. At school, I frantically searched ahead in the health book to find some answers. My period had stopped, and I literally thought I was pregnant. (Did I mention I was naive?) To my relief, I realized that was not how you get pregnant, and a short time later, my period returned again.

I hid in my pain for over four years before telling anyone and only dared to share it with a school girlfriend because she was moving out of town. There wasn't anyone I felt close enough to for me to tell. Not at my school. Not at my church. Not in my family. It was not their fault. I didn't know how to open up. The feeling of being alone was bigger than I had ever felt before.

That was the end of him and pretty much any other male! I hated his guts! I made sure I never stood close to him. I wouldn't speak to him. I wouldn't look at him. I wanted nothing to do with him. I wanted nothing to do with any male unless there was a large group of people around. The walls of protection around me went up very fast to make sure nothing like that would ever happen to me again. Thankfully he left for college soon, and I could breathe a sigh of relief. He was gone, but I kept up my guard by hanging an invisible sign on my heart, "No boys allowed!"

> I kept up my guard by hanging an invisible sign on my heart, "No boys allowed!"

CHAPTER 3

The Smiling Superhero

Beginning of Junior Year

Minnesota

Summer 1980

The sun's early morning rays threatened my precious teenage slumber. I was not fond of mornings, so I quickly rolled to my stomach and pulled the pillow tightly over my head to hide from the light. It worked for a short time, but my attempts to reenter the dream world were no match for the noises of life on a farm. Having no air conditioning, I slept with the windows open most nights, hoping for some trace of air movement to bring a little relief from the humidity and summer heat. Many nights, it would take a while to fall asleep. About the time I would be drifting off, a huge beetle would torpedo against the screen, scaring me and jolting me to fully awake status. Finally, I would calm down again and become tired enough to fall asleep to the crickets' lullaby and Frankie Valli's *Greatest Hits* playing *Big Girls Don't Cry* quietly on the record player.

Reluctantly, I crawled out of bed, remembering it was mowing day. My farmer father would pray for rain for the crops to grow while I would pray for rain to put off the mowing one more day. Obviously, my logic was flawed, as each summer's rain would make the grass grow much faster. Mowing really was not too bad. I loved the smell of fresh-cut grass, and the time spent on the mower was relaxing. It gave me plenty of time to think while working nearly all day to complete the job. I decided to make the most of it and headed outside to get started.

The two-story farmhouse, yellow with brown trim, sat back from the road in the middle of a large horseshoe driveway. It was perfect for our Sunday afternoon football games when some of my siblings were home. The one drawback was the tall flagpole positioned a little off-center but usually right in the middle of a really good play. Along one side of the driveway were well-manicured bushes spaced perfectly to practice running hurdles. This was much easier once they had been trimmed, but it was still a fun challenge to see who could get through the course with the least amount of scratches.

On the outside of the horseshoe, toward the east, was a beautiful apple orchard with over a dozen trees. Climbing up as high as I could, I would often hide in one of the trees and see how many green apples I could inhale before dinner without getting sick.

There was a large garden where I spent many nights as a child helping my mom patiently water each row. Growing older, I decided that was not as much fun as it once had been. The garden was stunning and produced an abundance of potatoes, carrots, onions, chives, cucumbers, tomatoes, and asparagus, which would be accidentally mowed down periodically to avoid having it served for dinner. The rhubarb was not my favorite either, nor did I enjoy mowing around the patch because snakes liked to hide under the large leaves.

On the other side of the horseshoe to the west were several rows of mature trees, an awesome playhouse that I enjoyed as a child, a horseshoe game area, and a tetherball game. Keeping that area mowed made it look nicer, but the threat of wood ticks was greater among all those trees, making it my least favorite part of the job.

Around the back of the horseshoe driveway were the buildings where we kept the farm equipment, a fenced area for horses (all of which were sold after my siblings graduated), gorgeous flower gardens, and a basketball hoop positioned over a grassy area (which did not assist my dribbling practice). As a kid, the farm seemed to go on and on forever. All this was bordered with a row of magnificent evergreen trees. It was picture-perfect, meticulously cared for, and a wonderful, peaceful place to grow up.

On this particular mowing day, I was thinking about the upcoming school year and looking forward to getting back to a schedule. Life could be rather lonely and boring in the country, but school brought with it plenty of opportunities for socializing. I was participating in a large variety of activities and excelled at whatever I did. One thing plagued me, however; I was not involved in the other kids' lives. I was not allowed to go to dances or movies. The only party anyone threw involved lots of beer, and I had made a decision in junior high not to drink. I had not made a public announcement, but people knew where I stood and seemed to respect me for it. I longed to fit in and be someone others would admire. In my fifteen-year-old brain, I wanted to be some type of superhero—to handle anything that came my way and to be a strong support to everyone; maybe then I would not feel so awkward around the other kids. When I was involved in basketball or music, there was a common focus, and I felt like I fit in—as long as the activity lasted. But outside of those activities, I found it difficult to relate to and connect with my peers.

In spite of my disengaged feelings, there was one school friend, Julie, whom I connected with. She had moved to our small town at the beginning of our seventh-grade year. One thing I was particularly gifted in was helping new students feel welcomed. Julie's dad was the recently-hired banker in town, so I had high hopes they would stay for several years. She had beautiful long black hair and a somewhat olive complexion. She was shy, but her smile was warm, and her laugh inviting. That would be my new goal—to make her smile and laugh—to help her belong.

Julie and I hit it off right away. We sang together. We played tennis together. We studied together. We swam together. We hung out at each other's homes. She was an only child, and for all practical purposes, so was I, with my siblings living many hours and states away. We became like sisters living in separate houses. Another common bond we shared was neither of us drank or attended the parties most of the kids our age went to. Finally, I had a close friend at my school!

There was a new Tri-county Christian Student Ministry (TCSM) that had started at our school a couple of years earlier. It was not connected with one particular denomination or church but would reach out to all the kids to build relationships with them and try to find opportunities to point them to Jesus. I was excited about this ministry. With our church so far away, I did not get to hang out with my Christian friends much. My hope was that this group would spark interest in Christianity and be a bridge for me to establish some deeper, more meaningful friendships at school. I had grown in reaching out to people, and I wanted to also be a witness for Jesus to the kids I spent the majority of my time with.

As I drove round and round and round our yard, mowing as straight a line as I could, I contemplated my character and who I wanted to be. Although I was involved with our church's youth group, it did not touch any of the kids' lives I saw on a daily basis. I wanted to make a difference in their lives, but I was not sure what I could do. I was already an advocate for the biweekly meetings of TCSM, and once in a while, I would invite someone from school to my church youth group meetings. I speculated if there was more I could do to be an encouragement to the kids and teachers in my school. I wanted to make a difference in their lives and be a superhero to point them to Jesus.

I began thinking about Jesus' life and how He effectively touched others in such a personal way. I wondered if I could do what He did as I recalled various Bible stories. I was curious about what Jesus did to reach out to people and meditated on what it was about Him that drew others close.

- Jesus cared and was kind to people regardless of their situation.

    I could do that.

- Jesus asked lots of questions, which showed He cared.

I could do that.
- Jesus hung out with people, looking past their differences to see their needs.

I could do that.
- Jesus offered hope when things seemed hopeless.

I could...wait...could I do that?

If something really bad happened to me, it would be a challenge to wear a smile and offer hope to others. I questioned myself if I could still be a witness, even if I had a disease. It was not like I really wanted to be sick, but if something horrible occurred in my life or the lives of those around me, I pondered if I would be strong and truly a witness through the difficult thing.

I imagined telling kids and teachers why I had hope. I decided smiling would help me reach out to them. Maybe if I smiled, they would see something different in me, or it might make me more approachable. So I began to practice right there on the mower. I must have looked like a real dork riding along, smiling as big as I could—just to practice.

Life went on, and I soon forgot about that day on the mower. Something bad did happen. In fact, a lot of bad happened— that year and a few years to follow. But I did not do a very good job pointing people to Jesus. I thought I was growing and doing pretty well in my young Christian life, but all of it was about to come crashing down. My superhero status was about to be compromised!

CHAPTER 4

The Frog
in the Kettle

Junior to Senior Years
Minnesota
1981–1982

My junior year was going to be the best! I just knew it. After long summers on the farm, I looked forward to getting back to school. Those seemingly unending months had brought about some disappointment. My friend from church, Sharon, had moved away and taken with her our special Sunday afternoon talks. Although I would terribly miss seeing her at church, I decided to focus on school activities and work on deepening friendships there. Most of my time was spent with Julie, and we were the best of friends. I did not see that ever changing. Here's to a new year of great memories—or so I thought.

Following my practice all summer on the mower, I anxiously anticipated trying out the new theory of connecting with people through smiling. I had high hopes of being more of an encourager, getting a greater number of kids to attend the TCSM meetings, and building closer friendships. Only two years left in that little town, and I wanted to make the most of it.

In a small school, there were opportunities to be involved in almost anything without any tryouts because they needed everyone who was even remotely interested just to make a team. My involvement with music, sports, and various clubs kept me extremely busy. Along with my school endeavors, TCSM had begun practice for a musical. That group felt like a protected place for me to spend time with people outside of school events. I thrived and found safety in encouraging students and maintaining an active lifestyle, whether it was with TCSM or other academic activities. If I continued to be busy, I would not have to have those awkward moments with my peers when I did not know what to say. So I fluttered around like a butterfly from person to person, trying to brighten their day and inviting them to the next TCSM meeting. I did not have to stop and engage in conversation because I was always on the move and needing to get to the next thing.

My favorite activity was performing with a barbershop quartet, of which Julie was also a member. We had sung together since the seventh grade and grown in not only our vocal ability but also our stage presence. Barbershop songs offered many opportunities to cut up and bring a laugh to those listening, which often fell into my lap. I was able to connect with the crowd through song and enjoyed joking around while we sang.

Our quartet coach, Kris, was also the TCSM leader. She was close in age to my sisters, which enabled me to relate well with her. Her mentoring and friendship held a warm place in my heart due to how much I missed my own sisters. Kris was good friends with the choral and band teacher at school, Miss Abbie Johnson, who was about her same age and also helped with the TCSM activities. I spent many hours in the music room, not only practicing or in class, but I also taught band lessons to younger students three days a week. That gave me plenty of time to hang out with those two ladies who were becoming more like sisters to me. Our friendship was growing, despite the difference in age. At the time, my parents felt comfortable with the friendships I had developed with my Christian mentors. That allowed me freedom to attend concerts with them (having no curfews), to visit their families out of state over the weekend, and to spend a large amount of time with them in and out of school settings.

The school was contacted often to have our quartet sing at a variety of community group meetings and nursing homes. We also had the privilege of singing on the radio, for city celebrations, and at Christmas banquets. Besides the local events, there was an annual statewide quartet competition in the spring that we were excited to enter. There would be workshops held throughout the day with well-known musicians giving us professional coaching. The weekend would culminate with barbershop quartets from all over Minnesota competing for the grand prize. The winners of the competition would return the following year to perform on TV as reigning champions. Our eyes were set on the goal, and we worked tirelessly toward that end.

Spring came quickly, and we were as prepared as we could be for the harmonic challenge. It was a surreal and amazing opportunity. The stage, the lights, the cheering—our top hats and canes displayed a classy act as we sang our hearts out...the best performance we had ever given. All our hard work had paid off—we won the state barbershop championship and would return the following year with our heads held high. Julie and I would be seniors, and although the other two were graduating, we vowed to continue to practice and become better than ever for our encore performance. This musical championship was a big deal for our little school and us.

~ ~ ~ ~ ~

Life was going at its normal, crazy speed as everything was winding down for the school year. Prom, with all its fanfare, was now a memory. The spring music concert, including our last school performance for the quartet, was now behind us. Track and baseball had just finished their seasons. All that was left was baccalaureate, a couple more finals, and then graduation would bring this amazing year to a close. After that, my best buddy, Julie, and I would be seniors! We could already feel the excitement.

Baccalaureate went about like any other year. Seniors sang their final songs. A local pastor shared a very short message. Someone actually prayed in school—back when we were allowed to do that. It seemed early when the service ended, but I was glad to have an opportunity to go home and get some extra rest before my last finals. Everyone mingled outside the school for a while, sharing in the seniors' excitement for the upcoming week of graduation. Before I left, I stopped to talk to Julie and one of the graduates, Becky. They had decided to go into the next town to get something to eat and asked if I wanted to join them. It was tempting and sounded like it would be fun, but I chose to go home instead. That was a decision I would come to regret for a very long time.

About the time I was ready to go to bed, I received a phone call from one of my classmates. Her voice was shaking as she told me Julie and Becky had been in a terrible car accident. She did not have any other details, but she knew I would want to be aware of what was happening. Thanking her, I quickly hung up the phone. I began to pray in a whisper, "Lord, Jesus, please let them be all right." My hand was trembling as I dialed Kris's number. She lived in the town where the hospital was located, so I knew she could get there quickly and relay information back to me about their conditions. My parents heard the concern in my voice and rushed to see what had me so upset. They, too, began praying as we waited for the phone to ring. It felt like an eternity as I paced back and forth, praying like never before. Finally, after a torturously long delay, the phone rang.

Kris's voice was quiet and somber, "Marilyn, it's not good."

I wanted answers, and I wanted them now! "What do you mean it's not good? What happened? Where were they? Are they okay? Are they being admitted? Can we see them? Should I come over there?" I did not even give her a chance to answer. I was so anxious to get some information, and she was not talking fast enough for me.

Kris tried to calm me as she began to give me the update. "The accident was at the three-mile corner. They were hit extremely hard because their car ended up in the northwest field." Kris took a deep breath before she continued, "Becky has some broken bones, one of her lungs has collapsed, and she is pretty banged up. It looks like she will be in here for quite a while. They may have to transport her to a larger hospital, but they are getting her stabilized before they make that decision. It will be a long recovery, but they think she is going to pull through."

I was trying to pay attention to every detail, yet my mind raced with so many questions. I wanted the information about Becky, but I was so impatient to hear about my best friend. "And Julie? What about Julie? Is she okay?"

"I'm sorry, Marilyn. She didn't make it." Kris's words stung like a pain I had never known! My breath was taken away. How do I even respond to that?

"*No!*" Tears burst from my eyes, and I fell against the wall to keep from crumbling to the floor. "No, that can't be right! She can't be gone!"

"Marilyn, I'm so sorry." She paused to let me catch my breath. Then she continued, "Listen...Julie's parents have already left. I'm going to sit with Becky's mom until more family arrives. Then, I'll come over to your place, all right?"

As we hung up, the questions flooding my mind were flowing faster than I could even articulate. My parents hugged me as I tried to relay the information. They had waited beside me for answers, but they already knew by my reaction what had happened. Time seemed to stand still. We stood there crying, trying to grasp the horrible news.

The questions continued to fly at me like arrows—each one piercing my heart with every blow...why hadn't I gone with them? Why was I here, safe at home? Why did she have to die? Who would be my friend now? Why did she have to leave me? The questions kept coming. It was like a dam had broken, and my heart was spilling out, gushing all over. There were no answers. Just questions. More and more and more questions.

Since Julie's parents did not have any family in the area, my parents went to their home to give some support. I had contacted Abbie, so she came to be with me until Kris arrived later that night. My first reaction in that time of desperate loss was to go to the piano to try to find some comfort.

Sitting down to the keyboard, I played a few of my favorite songs. One in particular was stuck in my head. Just a couple of weeks earlier at the spring concert, Julie and I had sung the contemporary Christian song "Rise Again" by Dallas Holm. I could not get the words of the verse she sang out of my head...

> Go ahead, and bury Me
> But very soon, I will be free...
> 'Cause I'll rise again
> Ain't no power on earth can keep Me down
> Yes, I'll rise again
> Death can't keep me in the ground[1]

I knew these words were speaking of Jesus after His death on the cross, but they were also so true for Julie in that moment.

I sang those words over and over as best as I could through my tears, trying to grasp the reality that the words my very best friend in the whole world had sung had actually come true. It was like a dream, and I really wanted to wake up!

"Please, someone, just wake me up!"

Kris arrived to my home later and decided to spend the night. She would be needed at the school the next day to be available to talk with students in the wake of the accident. It was an absolutely devastating loss for me. There were people close to me who had died, but this was a punch to the gut that would take years to work through. I did not know if I would ever get over it.

I could not have made it through the next few weeks and months without Kris. She was around day and night to talk to and listen to me and cry with me and listen some more. She never tired of hearing me share stories about Julie but allowed me to retell them over and over again. She also helped me work through the guilt I carried. My thoughts would get stuck on replay as I often wondered, *What if I had gone with them? What if I had seen the other car coming? Could I have stopped the accident? Would Julie still be alive?* Something inside me died that day right along with my dear friend. My hopes and dreams, my desire to encourage people and build relationships, my drive and purpose for living—it all seemed to be covered with a veil. I went through the motions of life, but everything was a fog.

The dog days of summer slipped by without noticing I was sitting on the sideline of life. Everything seemed to come to a screeching halt, and there was no way to get it moving again. All the anticipation and joy I carried the previous summer were nowhere to be found. As my senior school year began in the fall, the principal and teachers were very gracious and patient with me, as I would often run out of class crying or fall apart emotionally, never making it to class. Those were extremely difficult days for me. Life seemed so unfair as it continued on without her.

Life has a way of doing that—going on when you'd rather stop and get off the bus. Five months after Julie's death, my mom went into the hospital for one simple surgery and came out a week and a half later, having had multiple surgeries. Cancer does not wait for a good time to show up. This was the beginning of my senior year of high school, and I could not get more numb than I already was. Mom was very sick from the cancer treatments, staying in bed while Dad did what he could to keep things as normal as possible. He had to harvest the crops (with some much-needed help from a neighboring farmer), but after the harvest he would be free to care for her full-time for the winter.

Zoning out, I entered into my own little world, doing what needed to be done but handling everything with control and protection around my heart. Nothing was going to get in and hurt me ever again. I got myself up and off to school. I kept up my grades, kept up the sports, kept up responsibilities, and walked around in an inner daze. Staying busy, I learned quickly, was the key to keeping it all together. If my mind was focused on something else, I would not have time to reflect on how life was falling apart all around me. I was president of my senior class, president of the Future Homemakers of America club, played piano for our high school choir, and on and on. I had mastered the art of distraction.

My siblings were scattered across several states, and none of them really knew how badly I was hurting. I did not even think to bring it up with them. It was a very vulnerable, scary time for me, but Kris was my rock, my stability in all the turbulence I had walked through. Thankfully, I had her to watch out for me and be there for whatever I needed. Prior to that year, I had been growing spiritually and sharing often at youth group out of the overflow of what God had taught me by spending time in the Word. In the midst of all that pain, I continued to show up to the youth group, but I no longer felt engaged. I became skilled at going through the motions and keeping up the appearance that everything was okay.

My whole world had been turned upside down. My best friend (the only friend I hung out with) was dead; my joy of singing barbershop had been stripped away (two of the girls graduated, and Julie was gone); my parents were wrapped up in the health of my mom (as they should have been). School was a blur—I went and did what I needed to do, but I was walking in blindness, detached from much of what was going on around me. Kris was close at hand much more both at school and at my home. She would spend the night, give me rides, be with me when my parents were gone to the doctor, and on and on. I had not realized the void she filled with her presence, the

> I had not realized the void she filled with her presence, the peace she brought to my storm, and the comfort she gave to my obscurity.

peace she brought to my storm, and the comfort she gave to my obscurity.

Early in the spring of my senior year, I awakened from my vegetative state long enough to briefly wonder if something was not quite right in my relationship with Kris. I questioned my judgment, knowing I was not thinking straight much of the time. I felt so alone. I did not quite understand what was happening, nor did I feel I had the mental capacity to sort things out effectively. I tried to think back to months gone by—times I would wake up with her arm or leg flung across me or lying awkwardly close. Having grown up with siblings sleeping in the same bed, I did not really think too much about it at the time; after all, it was freezing in that house without insulation. Was there something that happened early on that I should have caught on to? Was I just not paying attention? Was that normal, or at what point did it quit being normal? The extended hugs. The back rubs that felt so good, and yet there was an uncomfortableness about them. Something was not right, but was I making it all up in my head? Was I going crazy? I could not deal with any of that at the time.

Slippery slopes propel you faster and farther than you ever imagined you could go. As graduation drew near, I realized that what she was doing was not right. There were times I would begin to wake up with her touching me very close to what would be inappropriate, and yet having the vague sensation that she may have already gone where she should not have been. Was she taking advantage of me in my sleep? I would lie still and try not to move, hoping I was wrong and that she would soon roll over. But time and time again, it would continue—and then, before long, I began to participate. I knew I should not be involved intimately, yet, it felt so good to be loved. The guilt and shame of realizing what I was doing weighed heavy against the physical and emotional comfort it brought me. I wanted to just crawl back into my fog and pretend it was all a dream. I did not know what to do to get out of this situation.

Kris was eight years older than me, served in a ministry organization, and had a strong personality. There was no thought or knowledge of a homosexual relationship running through my head at the time. Although I had grown a little older since my last encounter with molestation, I was still very naive. It was a classic case of "the frog in the kettle." I was beginning to boil to death and had no idea the very person I thought I could trust had not only turned the heat on but slowly intensified the temperature to dangerous levels as I became more lethargic. I did not realize it then, but I was being groomed for a homosexual relationship through her patient molestation in my vulnerable state.

Who would I go to now? Significant people in my life were gone, dead, or possibly going to die, and I did not want to lose another person whom I thought was an extraordinary friend. Then I would be all alone—again.

CHAPTER 5

From Victim to Choice

Early College Years
Minneapolis, Minnesota
1982–1983

Moving away to college left me feeling displaced. I did not have the normal excitement of beginning that new chapter in my life. In fact, life became more lonely as I lived in fear of what might happen if anyone realized the truth. But what was the truth? Was I gay? Was I lesbian? Was there a difference? I did not even understand the vocabulary, much less know if that was the kind of life I wanted. Still reeling from the pain of the last year, I stumbled through trying to decipher new terms, new feelings, and the overwhelming weight of not knowing where I fit. I could not imagine bringing up these questions with the few college kids I had recently met and with whom I had absolutely no connection. Unsure of what questions to even ask, I found myself withdrawing from people more and more. The scary part was no one seemed to notice. What was becoming of me?

Kris and I did not discuss what was happening in our relationship at all. She had moved to Minneapolis, yet there was still a pull to be near each other. Part of me hoped the distance between us would help to put an end to the physical side of the relationship. She was still my best friend, my only close friend, and I was lost without her. When we were together, I wanted to be close and intimate, yet deep inside, I thought I should not be wanting that. The inner battle was so confusing.

My mind was not on school or learning or meeting new friends. All I wanted to do was find a ride to Minneapolis to get away from everything unfamiliar at college and find my peaceful place with her. Although the peace was superficial, it was all I knew. It had become more comfortable to be with Kris, even with the confusion, than with anyone else. Because of the nature of the relationship, it was more acceptable and safe to be alone when we were together—which drew me farther away from people. Beginning to shift from the innocent, vulnerable victim of her schemes, I became a willing participant. I was making choices to stay in the game—a game I didn't know if I really wanted to play, but a player nonetheless.

> I found myself withdrawing from people more and more...no one seemed to notice.

I began playing piano for a singing group that performed at coffee shops and churches. The group's name, "70 × 7," came from the Bible story where Peter asked Jesus, "How many times must I forgive? Seven times?" Thinking he had gone over and above the normal duty of forgiveness, he awaited Jesus' affirmation. But Jesus replied, "Not seven times, but seventy times seven!"[2] As the story behind our group's name was shared at each concert, God planted seeds in my heart that slowly began to grow. Forgiveness, Jesus' love for us, and our need to love Him and others were themes woven through every concert. Little did I know, God watered those seeds each time we were together.

As we gathered in a circle to pray after weekly practice sessions, there was always a time to share about life and specific prayer requests. I admired the others who seemed to talk openly about struggles and needs in their lives. There was no way I would dare to say a word. I had to keep up the facade and continue to pretend everything was fine in my world.

God began speaking to me through times of reading the Word together and hearing different band members share during the concerts. They explained what God was teaching them and nuggets of truth they found in the Bible. My heart was heavy with the hatred I still carried for the young man from my church who had molested me. I sensed God nudging me. Was He really asking me to forgive the guy? How would I do that? How *could* I do that? Did I *want* to do that?

"Jesus, couldn't we deal with some gossip or maybe a bad word I've said here or there? What about going to church more? Or tithing? I would rather work on any of these things instead of forgiving!"

God's word has a way of piercing through the hardness of our hearts. There were so many things at this point that needed to be straightened out in my life, but He graciously began with one. It was a tough one, but at least it was just one.

"Lord, is my forgiving him saying I will forget what he did?

"'Cause I don't think I can do that!

"And is my forgiving him saying what he did was okay?

"'Cause it's not, and I can't ever believe that it was okay!

"And is my forgiving him saying that I have to be nice to him and talk to him and let my guard down?

"'Cause I don't think I can do that either!

"Are You sure this is such a good idea, God? Do You really know what You're asking me to do?"

Throughout the year, His gentle voice continued to whisper for me to forgive. The Lord and I had many arguments and battles inside my head over that topic. But I was learning to trust Him with a very tender, wounded part of my life. That very painful area was one I had kept hidden and locked away for years. Why would He ask this of me right now?

Finally, I made the decision to obey God. I wanted to be free from the prison I had placed myself in by carrying the heavy burden of unforgiveness for years, but it would involve the difficult task of letting go. Once I had made my decision to forgive, God put the pieces together. I had heard that the young man was visiting my college town for the weekend and would be driving back to Minneapolis a couple of days later. That was exactly where I wanted to go. If I rode with him, I could say what I needed to say privately without others being around. For some reason, I did not want to embarrass him or myself.

I could confront him one-on-one, and then, I would be done with it once and for all—hopefully.

The three-hour ride was awkward, to say the least. We were getting close to my drop-off point, so I knew I had to make my move soon. With my heart racing, I began...

"Jack, I have hated you for the last seven years, and I think you know why."

He became visibly very tense. His eyes were fixed straight ahead. He gave a little nod but did not say a word. So I continued.

"God's been telling me I need to let go of this anger. So I want you to know I am choosing to forgive you."

Not. One. Word. He didn't speak; he didn't move; he barely blinked. I am not sure he was even breathing at this point! We soon arrived at my destination, and we parted ways. I said good-bye and laid my burden down as I walked away—no longer carrying the mental weight of hatred toward him.

"Whew! All right, God, I did it! I'm glad that is over!"

I had done what God had asked me to do. Now I could go spend the weekend with my female lover in peace.

~ ~ ~ ~ ~

I do not know how God sorts out all our sin to guide us through the maze of our entangled, messy shortcomings, but I do know He led me to forgive that young man because it was *nothing* I would have come up with on my own! Even in my sinfulness, Jesus showed me a glimpse of truth, and He asked me to follow in this one little (okay, huge) area. There was still this issue of homosexuality, although I could not see through the smoke screen of lies to what I was doing and where this lifestyle was headed. There would be more steps of obedience in years to come, but not right now. I had done what I was asked to do, and life would have to play out some more for me to be able to recognize my need to obey again.

I often wonder and stand in amazement at God's patience and grace! Many people would have pointed out the homosexuality as something to deal with first because they often tend to categorize it as a worse sin. But God seemed to step right past that and choose to work on an area no one could see and very few even knew existed. It was a baby step for me, but He is delighted with our baby steps![3]

~ ~ ~ ~ ~

That weekend, as well as many others, I would escape my confused, lonely life at college and choose to walk deeper into the trench I had so comfortably slid into. There was no longer the same manipulation of my will. The decisions I made were definitely toward this new lifestyle. No longer did I wonder what was going on. I fully knew and embraced it, although there was an emptiness deep down that I had learned to disregard. As long as we could be in hiding and our relationship could stay a secret, I was good with this.

Periodically, though, there was a little gnawing in my gut. Something in my spirit was trying to cry out, "Stop!" I became proficient at ignoring it. Sin's pathway seemed to be widening, and the trail was so inviting. My decision-making and discernment became clouded as I continued down unknown paths. There were times I even risked my life trying to get to Minneapolis just to be with Kris at any cost.

I was borrowing a car from my parents at the time. My father had asked me not to take the vehicle to Minneapolis anymore because he noticed I was putting on a lot of mileage. I wanted to be a good daughter, so I agreed. But I was already scheming my other options, continually searching out a ride. Thankfully, I had the next one secured.

Although my ride was scheduled to leave in the morning, I had a brilliant idea to try to leave a few hours earlier. At "70 × 7" practice, I had asked one of the women in the band what she thought about me hitchhiking to Minneapolis. Needless to say, she was not impressed. She made me promise I would not do it. Having seen her reaction, I knew better than to bring up my next amazing idea with her—I would ride my bike!

It was late October in the north country. Although no snow had fallen, the chill in the air let me know it would come soon. I had my bike, a backpack, a warm jacket, and a determination to make it. One thing I had forgotten to check, though, was the batteries in the flashlight. It was the only light for the bike, and the batteries were about to die, so I would have to use it sparingly. I tried to ignore the fact that it was pitch black on the country roads, and, with no moon, my adventure seemed rather risky. But I was willing to do anything to get to Kris even a little earlier than if I waited for my ride the next day.

My roommate heard about my plan and knew she could not stop me. She offered to drive me to the edge of town, giving me at least a little head start down the road. It was 11:00 p.m. when we packed the bike into her trunk and headed out. She really was a great friend and offered to take me a little farther. And a little farther. And a little farther. She ended up driving me over a half hour down the road before she dropped me off in the black of night to start my overnight journey.

Driving this route would normally take three hours. As I struggled to pedal into the next town, I checked my watch, barely making it six miles down the road. Another half-hour had flown by, and it was freezing! There was no way I would be able to make it. I would have to swallow my pride, ask my roommate to come back to get me, and wait until the morning for my ride to Minneapolis.

Tiny farm towns in the middle of nowhere with populations of forty-five do not have much happening at midnight. I finally found a home with a light on and knocked. When the man came to the door, my story sounded much worse out loud as I tried to explain it to him. This was long before cell phones, so I asked to use his phone to make a long-distance call to get ahold of my roommate. The only problem was she had stopped to get gas and had not gotten home yet. So I sat down and waited while he watched late-night TV. I got through to her right before the man's girlfriend came home from working at the town's bar. Needless to say, I waited for my roommate's ride outside in the cold.

I was able to catch a ride to Minneapolis the next morning and arrived safe—unlike the thoughts that had gone through my head the night before. The road paralleled the railroad tracks, and I fought off the fearful idea of being thrown into a ditch somewhere. My passions were drawing me with great force. My mind became fuzzy, and my decisions were blurred. Like an addiction leading me astray, what I wanted became more important than my mental health or physical safety. That's the

> deceit —
> distorting the
> truth for the
> purpose of
> misrepresentation

way deceit works—distorting the truth for the purpose of misrepresentation.[4] You jump on this train that promises to take you to a perfectly sane, blissful destination—only to be fooled and whisked off to a world of delusion.

CHAPTER 6

Changes — Ready or Not

Late Teens
Minnesota to Colorado
1983–1984

Life was spinning out of control. At times, I thought I should stop this relationship, but how? And did I really want to? Maybe attending a Bible school would bring some clarity and be a good influence on me. So I decided to move to Saint Paul to pursue a degree from a Christian university and to surround myself with believers, although I did not have much support with the idea of attending college. I had been told, "Girls just go to college to find a guy to marry." That wasn't going to happen—at least it did not seem like a possibility since I was involved with a female. But I would have settled for a miracle where I could get my life back to some type of normal—whatever that was.

The relationship with Kris was like an obsession. Enticed by this person whom I questioned whether I should be involved with, I drifted further and further away from the reality of college life and a future career. I wanted the security of being with someone who loved me, who would take care of me, and who wanted the best for my future. Finally, I conceded to the battle for my heart and mind. Bowing out of college, I abandoned my search for God in singing groups, churches, or Christian higher education. I separated myself from people who did not understand nor have time for my confusion. We moved where we could hide—apartment managers barely had to leave home. Unfortunately, that meant I would be a prisoner of the building. No outside friends. No outside work. Still feeling like I did not fit in anywhere, I slowly isolated myself from people and had little to no contact with my family. What once was so important to me was lost as I sought to define family in a new way.

Amidst the loneliness, Kris always brought life to my day and lifted my spirits. Lately, she had been attending some meetings and coming home very excited. One night, I went with her to the meeting and was shocked at what I saw. There were cross-dressers and other people that I, as a naive farm girl, really did not feel comfortable with. Kris was checking into possibilities of us having a life together—a future—forever. I was uncertain of the changes and preferred to pretend our life was fine the way it was and that none of the rest of that uncomfortable part was even happening. She continued to research while I continued to just exist in that old building's basement apartment with little sunlight and deepening depression.

Having reached some conclusions about our next steps, Kris approached me with a proposed plan. She asked what I thought about her becoming a man so that we could be married. My processing of that information was in slow motion. "Wow! Wait, what? Is that even possible?" Could I finally have the family life I longed for? At that moment, I was not looking at how I would get that family—I was only focused on the end result of one day belonging in a family. My denial of reality went unchallenged since my contact was limited to Kris and an occasional check-out person at the grocery store. She was my main connection to the outside world and had tapped into this new possibility where I could have what I wanted with a family and no more pain.

> My denial of reality went unchallenged...

Once the idea of being a family sunk in a little, I began to get excited. The first order of business was to pick a new last name. She thought it would be best to hide under a fictitious name so people would have difficulty finding us. Opening the three-inch thick phone book, she began calling out names that sounded good. What seemed like a genius idea for us to begin a new family brought with it absolutely no family connections. Yet, we continued the search for a name... "Anderson?" No, that is too common. "Carter?" No, that is not good. "Fontaine?" I liked the sound of that. Someday we would be Mr. and Mrs. Fontaine.

Kris was moving forward with preparing for change, but I still seemed to be stuck in the fog of my pain and depression. Not only would there be a name change and marriage, but we would be moving to Colorado to start our new life together.

There was not a forcing of this on my will, but I went along with it like there was no option. What I really wanted was a life where I could be free to love and show affection to my husband—a life where I was safe and secure with someone who loved me and would not leave me like everyone else had done—a life where there was a future with a family. There were other things Kris was working on regarding the big change, but I did not really want to know about those. All I wanted was to live in my fairy-tale world where I could pretend everything was magical. The name change, gender change, and surgeries would proceed once we moved out of state.

As I struggled mentally and emotionally, my attempt to prepare for living in a new state consisted of imagining being in the mountains. Colorado sounded like an exciting place to live. I loved the mountains and looked forward to spending time in them. Whether hiking, skiing, or exploring the back roads, the mountains made me feel closer to God. That was something I knew I needed—a connection to God.

The communication with my family had slowed down to almost none. My parents had traveled out of state to their winter retreat, and my siblings were still scattered across the country. When we moved, there would be no one for me to say good-bye to. After Kris finalized things with the property manager she was working for, it was just a matter of packing up a few things, loading the furniture into the pint-size U-Haul, and leaving. It would be a strange feeling to walk away from the state I had called home for all my growing-up years. My hope was wrapped up in the fantasy of starting over with a life that would somehow be acceptable and perfect.

While I had not done any research on life in Colorado, Kris continued to encourage me, saying there were great opportunities for us there, so I believed her—without question. This would be a chance to start our lives afresh with doctors who could help her change from a female to a male. Then we could be married and be together forever. I focused on the only part I was interested in...happily ever after.

The whole thing was overwhelming and very scary, maybe because I was not well informed or maybe because I was living in denial of what was really going on. I wanted to be married. I wanted a family of my own. I wanted to marry a man. Yet, I was still scared of men, and furthermore, I was caught in this dilemma of loving a woman who loved me and was taking care of me. Life had turned so unpredictable after Julie's death that the relationship, though I questioned it in my head at times, was the only stable thing in my life.

That stability had, as its foundation, a lie that we fabricated. I was desperately trying to believe it and make it come true because—it was my only hope. Everything in me wanted the change in Kris and the marriage to somehow work out to be good, with everyone I knew accepting it, loving me, and congratulating me. We would finally be a family like everyone else.

The lies had begun even with the minimal contact with my family. I had previously been interested in interpreting for the deaf, and the University of Northern Colorado in Greeley offered a deaf education degree that would fit perfectly into our story. My parents and family were told about my new-found career goals and the move to Colorado. Kris had friends in the state of Washington and would drop me off on her way to the West Coast. At least that was the story I told them. The web of lies I began weaving was somewhat energizing. I could make myself out to be something I wasn't, but deep inside, I wished I could be. Strong. Confident. Pursuing a future and a career. The complexity of the lies grew as I had to remember what had been said. Minnesota would soon be in the rear-view mirror. Maybe then the ache in the pit of my stomach would ease up a bit.

~ ~ ~ ~ ~

Colorado is beautiful any time of year, but it is especially beautiful in the winter. Life was harder than I had anticipated. Counting pennies to buy bread and milk. Finding pop cans to take to the recycle bin just to get a little change to buy a donut. Paper routes at 3:00 a.m. *Tell me why we were doing this again.*

Considering I was so unsure of my behavior and the direction we were headed, in the courtroom of my mind, I chose to plead ignorance, insanity, or anything that would take away my responsibility. Kris continued to make contacts and began to establish her new life transitioning to a man. She was able to find a job that allowed her to work

> ...in the courtroom of my mind, I chose to plead ignorance, insanity, or anything that would take away my responsibility.

independently and hide her real identity while beginning the hormone treatment process.

My confidence was at an all-time low. How did I go from high school's "Most Likely to Succeed" to this? I felt like I was the scum of the earth, far beneath others, and scared to try anything. A couple of part-time jobs helped to plant a seed of courage. Soon thereafter, I landed a job I could grow in for the next year. It was a relief to be moving in a positive direction. My boss was the toughest administrator in the company, but I learned so much from her. She knew what she wanted when she asked for computer reports that I did not know how to produce, and she would not allow me to settle into, "That can't be done." Her drive forced me to work harder, finding ways to accomplish what she needed. I enjoyed getting out and being around other people at work. There was a glimpse of my old self beginning to sprout. It was almost like being back in high school again, where I thrived on encouraging people. That felt really good.

Changes continued to take place on the home front. The ideas about a new name, a new gender, and a new identity were beginning to take shape. I still chose to keep my head in the sand about much of it. It did not seem so bad if I wasn't aware of the details. If I could flip the mental switch in my head to pretend and really begin to believe she was actually a "he," then everything in life would work out. The more I told myself black was white, the more I believed it. Truth was shifting.

Doubt and confusion continued to cloud my thinking. It was not a doubt of wondering if what we were doing was wrong. It was more a doubt of wondering if it could be right. If my heart's desire was to be married and the biggest hurdle was finding a Christian, then everything was good, right? (Other than the fact that she was female—but she was taking care of that little detail.)

Struggling to hang on to any part of my Christian upbringing, I tried to find something in the Bible to justify my actions. As I read the Genesis account of God creating male and female along with other scriptures about homosexuality, somehow I reconciled what I read with what I believed to be acceptable behavior; after all, we were good people. Little did I know that everything was becoming twisted in my head, and my understanding of what the Bible said was different than what I would later come to realize was truth. How could I read one thing and totally rationalize my thoughts and actions? The father of lies, Satan, tripped me up with his trickery and continued to slowly twist God's truth. The more I read, the more confused, backward, and twisted my thinking became. Satan's grip of deceit was tightening a bit more with each passing day.

> The more I told myself black was white, the more I believed it. Truth was shifting.

Since I had read my Bible some and was getting my life together, or so I thought, I wanted us to get back into church and build our lives together on a strong Christian foundation. Something in me was pulling me to find a church. If we were going to have a strong family, we would need to be involved in church life. We began attending a large Southern Baptist church during the middle of Kris's transition, but no one there knew our situation. There had been enough changes in Kris that she was able to pass as a man (a somewhat effeminate man, but for our purposes, a man nonetheless). The experiments of going out in public as a couple were working well, and either people were actually seeing her as a male, or they were too polite to say anything. The church was a better place to hide and move forward with our plans than I had originally thought because they accepted everyone. After all, no one at church was going to come up to her and ask if she was a man. We fit right into the singles group and proceeded on with life.

I was beginning to feel somewhat normal again. We began working with the children's ministry part time as well as helping in leadership roles within the singles ministry. That year had brought me a little further out of my shell. With our outgoing personalities, our strong ability to encourage, and past Bible teaching experience, we were quite a team. Someday soon, we would join together as a married couple—illegally, but no one at church knew our secret.

As we moved forward with each step, the secret became more twisted. At the courthouse, Kris indicated on the official name change document that she was "male" when she changed her last name to "Fontaine." There were no questions asked. Everything would be legal on paper but in reality, a lie. She would go by "he" and continue as "Kris," which no longer stood for her birth name, "Kristine." That was an easier process than we had expected.

The stress of carrying the secret was making life nearly unbearable at times. Thinking a career change would help, I began asking about job openings at our new church. They were doing some restructuring and just happened to have an office position available, which would work out great. I was getting back into a place where, for some reason, I felt safe—within the church. Although people had hurt me in the church, it seemed the safer choice than the outside world. Besides, it would look good to my family with me working at a church.

~ ~ ~ ~ ~

Finally, we began to plan our wedding. I was so excited to be able to join together in marriage with my best friend, yet there was an emptiness inside due to none of my family being able to share in our exciting news. The anxiety I experienced when I thought about breaking the news to them was enough to make me sick. It was almost debilitating, but there was a small ray of hope that I would be able to share it in such a way that they would obviously see it from my perspective and be overjoyed.

Sharing my wedding announcement with them sounded like a good idea at the time. I decided to phone my parents before sending them and my siblings the "tell-all" letter, which explained my relationship with Kris and the upcoming marriage. I practiced over and over exactly what I would say and replayed each expected response in my head until I had it down pat. All that repetition did not prepare me for what was to come.

Let's just say the conversation did not go as I had planned. I had never heard that kind of distress in my mom's voice—she was beyond devastated. Dropping the phone on the desk, she ran to the basement and left me hanging there, wondering what to do next. Her screams had been heard by Dad, who was outside on the mower. Not knowing what was happening, he ran to the phone to find out who had called and what had been said. Now I had to tell him. That was a much quicker, more painful moment. He had to leave quickly to check on Mom, so thankfully, that conversation was short.

My palms were sweaty when I hung up the phone, and my shortness of breath left me very light-headed. With all the tension and panic I was feeling, it took me a while to calm down. Once I did, there was almost a little sense of accomplishment that came over me. I had done a very hard thing, and even though it did not go as I had hoped, at least I told my parents that I was happy and moving forward. There had been a few years for my mind to be molded and my thinking to be convinced that this was right, but it hit them like a lead balloon.

The family letters were mailed the next day, and I quietly closed that chapter in my life. I did not know who I would hear from, nor did I know what to expect. With all that behind me, I took a deep breath and began to work on wedding preparations. There was plenty to do and never enough time to get it all done.

After a few days, my parents and some of my siblings began to respond to my correspondence. Whether I heard from them all or not, I do not remember. Some responses were somewhat neutral—not exactly excited for me, but not ugly either. Unfortunately, the much easier ones to recall are the ones with negative words that would ring in my head for several years. I do not remember exactly from whom they came, but what I remember communicated, "You're going to hell!" "You're not even saved!" "You're not acceptable!" "Jesus can't love you like that!" The exact words they wrote were not quite so harsh, I'm sure, but sadly, those thoughts played over and over as a recorded message I could not turn off.

Their letters, some with bitter words (whether perceived or actual), did nothing to draw me back to my family or a God, who now had to hate me. The one thing it did accomplish was to assure me it was the right decision to have cut off ties when I did. I would have to toughen up and put this behind me so I could focus on my wedding day—sadly, without them.

~ ~ ~ ~ ~

Everything was moving along and according to my plans until...my parents showed up. They had driven to Colorado to help me clear my head of this craziness and take me back to Minnesota. I remember thinking, *Take me back? To what? There is nothing back there for me!* They asked me to meet with them and a random Baptist pastor they had contacted. Surely he could help them knock some sense into me.

Our meeting was brief, and the outcome was not at all what my parents had hoped for. The pastor told them to let me be—it would not last forever. He said to let me walk through this, that I needed to know if I could do it, and he was sure it would all work out. From my parents' perspective, this pastor must have appeared absolutely insane. But I thought he was surprisingly pretty wise.

I am certain they felt completely defeated. After giving me until the next morning to make my decision, we said a quick, awkward good-bye. They would be leaving town but would wait for my call. Should I choose to go with them, I could leave immediately. Should I choose to stay, I would be disowned. (These exact words were not specifically spoken, but an underlying sense of being cut off was communicated.) They were helpless to rescue their little girl and did not know what else to do. Needless to say, it was a pretty sleepless night for me and, I'm sure, for them as well. I had had everything figured out until they showed up, but now I was even more confused than ever.

The next morning, I dreaded making that call. I loved them, but my heart had become so calloused, I was not thinking straight. There was not a lot of practice for this call. I just needed to get it over with. My heart was racing as I picked up the phone to give them my final answer. It was not pleasant. When all was said and done, I told them to leave town, never wanting to see them again in my life. I cannot even imagine the pain and grief in their hearts as they drove away, leaving me in Colorado that day.

I hung up the phone with enormously deep distress, an unfathomable agony I did not even know could exist, and a deluge of tears that left me gasping for air. How could I have treated my parents like that? Why did I have to choose? Would this dark cloud ever leave me? Hopeless and exhausted, I no longer wanted to live.

The emptiness in my heart was bigger and deeper than anything I had ever experienced. Lies and accusations swirled around my head until I could no longer take it. Maybe I could find some peace and make the battle in my heart and mind cease if I drove off a mountain road.

Still shaking from my sobbing cries, I ran to the car and headed toward the mountains. The drive was surreal. It felt like I was the only one on the road. I knew other cars were there, but I did not really see them. Around curves. Up hills. Dodging in and out of traffic. Mountain tunnels. Slow tractor-trailers. I have no idea how long I drove. I was going through the motions but had no recollection of how I arrived up on those twisting roads, weaving my way to nowhere in particular. It was a day I hoped would prove to be my last! That was the lowest I had ever been. The only answer—the best thing would be to just drive off one of those curves and end my life. That way everyone would no longer have to deal with the pain I was causing them.

> More than death, I just wanted the bleeding of my heart and the tremendous pain to stop!

Without knowing how, I was turned around and headed back down the mountain. Each curve brought with it a decision. Would this be a good one to go over the edge? I wanted to yank the wheel to the right, yet something was guiding my hands around each curve, keeping my tires on the road. I did not take that leap off the edge where I was longing to go that day. More than death, I just wanted the bleeding of my heart and the tremendous pain to stop!

Through an avalanche of tears, I somehow arrived back in town at my home. Why hadn't I gone through with it? Wouldn't dying make all this much easier? How did I even get down the mountain? Angels were on guard at each curve, guiding the turn of the wheel and giving that extra nudge I needed to keep me on the road. Life, with all its changes, would go on—whether I was ready for it or not.

CHAPTER 7

Imposter with a Bleeding Heart

Early Twenties
Colorado
1984–1985

The time in Colorado was the most desolate years I had ever experienced. Life seemed to be moving forward, yet there was an aloofness about me; I felt detached and paralyzed inside. I had successfully shifted Kris to male pronouns in my head, so I felt a little safer talking with people. Still, there was not a freedom to fully relax and let my guard down because if I did, I might give away our secret. Keeping everyone at bay and living cautiously became a way of life. My greatest fear was slipping up and saying something that would give away the fake life we had come to know. This award-winning performance was weighing heavy on my heart. There seemed to be no option but to just continue. For added protection, I closed myself off from my siblings for the next several years, hoping to stay safe in my make-believe cocoon. One sister and her family had attempted to find me while passing through the state but were unable to. I did not realize my family's pain nor how my hiding would affect them. Although my earthly family did not know my location, thankfully, I was never hidden from my Heavenly Father—who was lovingly pursuing me.

The wedding day finally came, and everything went smoothly, without a hitch. It was held at a beautiful location in a little chapel up on a mountainside. Many wonderful people from our church, who knew nothing of our lies, came to support us. Pastor Andy, one of the assistant pastors I worked with, officiated the ceremony. He, too, had absolutely no knowledge of Kris's real identity. Having met with Pastor Andy for marriage counseling,

> I was never hidden from my Heavenly Father—who was lovingly pursuing me.

nothing was ever brought up about the masks we wore or the truth behind them. We became so good at playing the game, it even surprised me at times. Everything was going as planned without any difficulty. As I walked around the venue after the ceremony in a bit of a daze, I kept telling myself, *Just keep going through the motions. Follow through with the plan. Keep calm because one slipup, and this could all be really embarrassing.* Never once did I allow myself to think or feel from the depths of my soul. There was an altered surface level I functioned on. If I could keep moving and not look back, I might just make it.

~ ~ ~ ~ ~

Life seemed to be falling into place. Work, home, time with friends...that was guarded time, but at least there were a few people who I called "keep-at-a-distance friends." Soon Kris and I were able to purchase our first home together. What a thrill it was to be living the American dream and to have something that was ours—together—husband and wife (well, kind of). Everything seemed to be going well, so why was I feeling this gnawing in the pit of my stomach? I could finally settle into married life and feel like I fit in. After such a long time of walking in complete darkness and feeling like an outcast, to at least be a family and belong was such a blessing. So why the discomfort?

The emptiness and loneliness grew heavier and darker every day. What was wrong? Wasn't this what I wanted? Living the lie was taking its toll on me. I began to shut down emotionally. I could not share with anyone what I was feeling. It felt like I began to die inside a little more each day. A church service, a prayer meeting, a Bible study—nothing could penetrate my heart. I was completely debilitated. Trapped in another prison I had built to protect myself, I was dying there with seemingly no way out.

I loved our church and the small sense of security I felt when I was there. As the hollowness grew inside, there also sprouted an unfamiliar hunger to learn more about the Bible. We continued to serve in the singles ministry and started a Bible study. Kris held one for the guys, and I led the young ladies. These young women and I were hungry for the Word, and it became a sweet time of growth and support for each of us. I was encouraged as we studied, yet I could not be real. My desire to open up and share my heart would attempt to surface at times, only to be quickly stuffed back down in the pit of my deep, dark secret. The witness protection plan I had put myself in was difficult, but I was learning to manage it rather well.

> Trapped in another prison I had built to protect myself, I was dying there with seemingly no way out.

The heaviness that came along with hiding was totally draining. Most of the time at work, I had little contact with people, which made it easier. But on Mondays, there was an amazing group of ladies who would volunteer in the church office. About eight to ten of them would show up each week to help with whatever needed to be done. They assisted with many office tasks—visitor contacts, attendance, new member follow-up, and entering the financial contribution details into the computer. I worked closely with two of them weekly and wished I could get to know them better, but there was always a veil I kept up between myself and others.

"Lord, I'd love for You to tear that screen down someday, but I just can't risk it now."

One of the most memorable things with this group of volunteers was our lunch times together. The pastors, secretaries, office help, and volunteers would gather around a pot of stew or something delicious someone had brought in to share. It was fascinating to me to watch how they interacted with each other. Because of my guarded life, I loved observing people, wishing I could take part in the fun. I was held captive inside my cautious lifestyle, watching others laugh, tell stories, and share life together. Would I ever be able to come out of this protective bubble and share in true community?

Excitement grew at our church as a new pastor soon arrived to shepherd us. Pastor Jonathan was an excellent pastor, and his smile and laugh were contagious. Both he and his wife had a great love for people and a strong belief that prayer changed things. Several months after their arrival, his wife initiated a weekly 6:30 a.m. gathering of the women on staff to pray before work. Wanting to fit in and show my interest in spiritual things, I joined them as often as possible. I had learned how to share vague prayer requests and pray without opening the vault to my real self. I thought I could pull this off.

Keeping up appearances is exhausting, and I soon became extremely weary of the game I was playing. So confused, I cautiously approached God to ask some questions. Sitting under the preaching of God's Word and spending time in prayer had created a crack in what I thought I had sealed tight. Truth was sprouting through my hardened soil.

"God, how do I live in submission to my husband's God-given authority and try to be a better wife to him when he's not really a man?

"And, Lord, how do I take what I'm learning through the preaching of Your Word and apply it when so much of my life is a mess?

"God, I'm scared to ask this, but do You really even see us as married?

"Do You have an opinion about this whole 'change' that is taking place, and if so, can You keep that part to Yourself and just teach me other stuff?"

~ ~ ~ ~ ~

Maybe I needed to get involved in some activities outside the church to give me a little break from God and all the questions. I had used the deaf education degree as a smoke screen for my family before moving to Colorado, but interpreting for the deaf really did interest me. I began taking some adult sign language classes at the community college. Our teacher was an older deaf gentleman who was involved at a deaf church and suggested we come to some of their activities to practice our signing. (I couldn't get away from church and God if I tried.) It turned out to be a lot of fun, plus I found two friends who made me laugh and forget about my crazy life. I was hooked.

Linda was taking the sign language classes with me, and Emily was an interpreter who served in leadership at the deaf church with her husband, Mark. She grew up with deaf parents and had been interpreting since before she could talk. These ladies taught me so much about friendship as we spent time together, enjoying each other's company as often as we could.

The companionship with these two was so enriching for me. Sometimes we would get away for the weekend to one of the hot springs in the mountains. Other times we would meet at a restaurant and drink coffee till the wee hours of the morning. Once in a while, we would find a ministry opportunity.

One of those particular times, we were asked to sign a song during a hearing church's revival service. Emily would sign the song while Linda, dressed in white, and I, dressed in black, battled in the background. As the song talked about the battle raging, Linda and I clasped hands and wrestled back and forth for control.

> There's a line that is drawn through the ages
> On that line stands an old rugged cross
> On that cross, a battle is raging
> To gain a man's soul or it's loss
>
> The earth shakes with the force of the conflict
> And the sun refuses to shine
> For there hangs God's Son, in the balance
> And then through the darkness He cries[5]

At the chorus, the battle would be over as Linda defeated me, and I fell to the ground with her hands raised in triumph depicting Christ's victory.

> It is finished, the battle is over
> It is finished, there'll be no more war
> It is finished, the end of the conflict
> It is finished and Jesus is Lord[6]

The second verse drew a picture of the battle that rages inside each of us. This was portrayed by two young kids also dressed in white and black, using the same battle moves as Linda and me. It was such a powerful song and gave such a clear, visible picture of the battle taking place inside my own heart.

Yet in my heart, the battle was still raging
Not all prisoners of war had come home
These were battlefields of my own making
I didn't know that the war had been won

Oh, but then I heard the King of the ages
Had fought all the battles for me
And that victory was mine for the claiming
And now praise His name, I am free[7]

Listening to this song talk about the battle raging inside was like someone portraying my heart on the big screen. The emotion was so strong and powerful, yet I was not free. I was still a prisoner in this battle "of my own making," and if the war was won, then somehow I had been left out on the battlefield.

"God, what is happening? Life is settling down for me a bit, and everything is lining up in its place for me to have a happy family. Why am I beginning to question all I have done now? Why can't I find any peace? Why is my heart racing when the chorus plays, 'It is finished, the end of the conflict'?"

He might have had a good answer to each of my questions, but I gave Him no time to respond.

"Conflict ended? No, it didn't, God! There is still plenty of conflict going on in here!"

"And what about the line, 'Victory was mine for the claiming'? Really? What does that exactly mean, God?

"So now what do I do?"

I loved getting together with those two crazy ladies who seemed to love me and accept me, although they had no idea about the secret life I was living. Our conversations were real—

well, not mine, but I believe theirs were. I was delighted to have found a place to belong. Now if I could only quiet this raging war within me. I had become an imposter of a good life, yet my heart was bleeding out.

MY JOURNEY
OUT OF
HOMOSEXUALITY

CHAPTER 8

War in the Heavenlies

Early Twenties
Colorado
1986

There were a handful of people at my church who had captured my attention. Although I could not allow myself to get close, I admired them from a distance. They had a genuine love for people and seemed to have an authentic relationship with Jesus. That was something I was unaccustomed to, and yet it invigorated me. There was something in their lives that was absent from mine, and I wanted it.

One lady in particular, Miss Ruthie, had a magnetic energy and loved Jesus with all her heart. She shocked me several times, as she would talk with people about Jesus outside of church events. When we were in public, she would grab my hand and pray before we ate. As she spoke to Jesus, it was like He was literally in the room with us. What was it that made her love Him and talk to Him like that? I wanted to know Him like she did.

Miss Ruthie was the children's minister at our church. I began hanging around her and anything connected to the children's ministry just to soak up as much information as I could about having a real relationship with Jesus. After cautiously observing for some time and slowly allowing myself to become a bit more vulnerable, I finally asked her to mentor me. I did not know exactly what that would entail, but I had heard people talk about it, and there was something she had that I knew I needed.

One of the places I was able to analyze and learn from her was when the staff ladies gathered for prayer. I did not always get much out of that time together, but I desperately wanted to show that I fit in with those who were spiritual and praying for the ministry at our church. After a few months of getting together, they announced we would be having a prayer seminar for the whole congregation. I had no clue what a prayer seminar was, but I did not want to appear unspiritual, so I did not ask any questions. There was a woman from Minnesota coming to speak about prayer and share how God had changed a small group of ladies through prayer. As the seminar approached, I became a little nervous about attending. What were they going to do? Would I be able to blend into the crowd? I carried a lingering fear that people could look at me and somehow know I was hiding and lying about something big in my life. I would definitely have to be careful at that event.

When I arrived on Saturday morning for the seminar, the chapel was already packed, and my nerves were on high alert. Part of me wanted to run and hide, yet I wanted to see what it was all about. What would the day hold? How could the guest speaker talk about prayer all day long? I sensed something big was going to happen, but I had no idea how much it would impact my life.

The guest speaker, Evelyn Christenson, was a middle-aged, grandmotherly lady. She smiled continuously, and there was something warm and inviting about her. Knowing she came from my Minnesota roots made me a little homesick, and I wanted to listen to what she had to say. She was a gifted speaker who easily drew me into her amazing stories of answered prayer. At times throughout the day, I would begin to sense I was letting my guard down, only to be jerked back into the reality that I needed to keep my distance emotionally. The examples of how God spoke through His Word to her and the group of ladies she met with were unbelievable. It was all very exciting, and I wanted to know more. Could God really do all that through prayer?

Later in the afternoon, there was a point where we split up in groups of three to pray. At first, I was scared. What if I slipped and said something I shouldn't? As we bowed to pray, I could feel something was happening deep inside me, but I could not quite put my finger on it. I had to keep reminding myself to keep up my guard, although I longed to be genuine.

When the seminar was over, I purchased all of her books and could not wait to get home to begin reading. I decided to start with *Lord, Change Me!*

"Jesus, can You really do that? Can You change me? Can You actually work in my heart and speak to me through Your Word and prayer? That lady said You wanted to and that You would draw me closer to You so I could know You better. Was all that for real?"

Part of me was scared of what I might hear Him say. Was He angry with me? What was He going to do to me if I got close to Him? So many questions plagued my mind. Although there was a fear of getting close to Him, a bigger part of me was longing for something more—something that I did not even know how to ask for. Curiosity got the best of me, and I decided to give it a try.

Soon I began getting up each morning at 4:30 a.m. I could not get enough. I wanted to learn so much more as I began to read from my Bible. There was a joy that seemed to flow from Evelyn and others from my church that I longed to have as a part of my life. Change seemed so out of reach and impossible. I thought I wanted to change, but I did not know how to achieve it. Nor did I know exactly what needed to change. God was more than willing to show up each morning and meet me through the time I spent in His Word. Little did I know all He had in mind.

> ...part of me was longing for something more— something that I did not even know how to ask for.

My prayers were simple, and I came with no expectations. Just like a child, I was eager to experiment and see if this would really work. I wanted to hear from God and catch a glimpse of what having a relationship with Him was all about.

In her book, Evelyn said she learned to hear God speak to her. She would read the Bible until He spoke through a word or phrase that seemed to jump off the page. This would become like a red flag, urging her to pause. Then, she would pray and ask God why He stopped her there and what He wanted to say to her through that verse. When she sensed Him speaking to her, she would write down whatever He said. God would begin to put together the pieces of what she had been praying about as He spoke through His Word. I had to try this!

"God, would You really speak to me? I know I asked You to forgive my sin and come into my heart a long time ago as a child, but I haven't been very consistent about living like a Christian. Can You speak to me too? How will I know it's You? Will I see You make certain words jump up at me? Will I be able to hear Your Spirit speak to me? Lord, change me!"

Ruthie and I had already been talking about hearing from God as we worked together on projects for the children's ministry. One of the things she encouraged me to do was to make sure my pipeline to God was open. She said, "Just like the downspout on the side of a house needed to be clear and not clogged up, my heart needed to be free from sin. I needed to confess my sin and ask God's forgiveness on a daily basis." Wow, I had a lot to confess. My pipeline felt pretty clogged when I talked to God in prayer. Sometimes, my prayers seemed to just bounce off the ceiling. I was desperate to connect with Him, so I determined in my heart to keep trying and do everything I was learning.

Early in the morning, I would quietly sneak out of bed and head to the living room. Laying face down on the floor with a warm blanket over my body and head, I would capture the heat from the register on the floor as I read. I was not sure where to start, but the Gospel of John was familiar, so I began there.

Amazed, I found that when I earnestly sought God, asking Him to reveal Himself and speak to me, He did. Each day, He began to show me something new. At first, it was observing an aspect of the chapter I had never seen before. Sometimes I read a few verses. Some days, I only read one. It was so exciting, I could hardly wait to get up to meet Him each morning.

Evelyn had said in her book to pray and then read until He speaks to you. Every day, I would follow that guideline, and each day, He was faithful to speak to me. After some time, He began to show me things in my life that needed attention. It was almost like looking into a mirror, seeing things that needed to be addressed. An attitude of jealousy. Maybe some pride. Daily, there seemed to be something new, and I soon began to get a backlog.

> He faithfully drew me to Himself and daily revealed His deep love for me. I could not stay away.

"God, wait a minute! I haven't fixed the thing You told me to fix yesterday or the day before or the day before that. Can You hold up a second and give me a chance to catch up?"

What was amazing to me was that God did not hit me with the whole idea of, "You're going to hell if you don't change your lifestyle." He was gentle. There were many things He was showing me to change, but it had nothing to do with my current lesbian situation. I did not think that needed to change. We were married. She was transitioning to a male. There was no longer a problem with that in my mind. If God had told me to change that right away, I probably would not have listened to Him anyway. But He faithfully drew me to Himself and daily revealed His deep love for me. I could not stay away.

Although I was spending time in the Word, trying to find joy for my life, the conflict in my heart continued to grow. I desperately wanted to be closer to Jesus and for my life to reflect Him. I wanted my Christian marriage to reflect what He called me to, but how could I do this when I was married to a biological woman who was pretending to be a man? There was a war between what I currently believed and what I somehow knew to be truth deep in my heart. The crisis grew stronger and brought on a heaviness I could hardly bear. Emotionally, I became a wreck. I could not eat. I barely slept. I was a volcano of feelings getting ready to explode. I had no idea how to handle all the things God was teaching me through His Word. My thought process was beginning to shift, and I did not know what to do.

"God, what do I do now? I've been taught You hate divorce. Is that right? So I'm trapped...living a lie. I cannot go forward living a married life to a transgender, and I cannot go backward, which would involve divorce. What do You want me to do?"

I was going crazy trying to figure it all out and yet keeping everything to myself. There was absolutely no one I could confide in at this level of vulnerability because I had made sure not to tell anyone about any part of our lifestyle choices. My questions were not anything I could discuss with Kris at the time due to the conflict that involved him. I felt like I was going to go insane.

I continued to get up early to meet Jesus on my face, prostrate before the Lord with my blanket covering to keep me warm. Seeking His heart became a great desire of mine, but I was not really sure I wanted to hear what He might say regarding this issue.

God was faithful and continued to meet me there—revealing truth after truth and unwrapping, layer by layer, many of the protective walls I had built around myself. I was getting ready to burst, but where and with whom and how and...what would happen next? It was more than I could take.

One day, as I arrived at work a little early so I could slip into my office without seeing anyone, I concentrated on working quietly—not wanting to speak with people but just focusing on my job. I felt if I looked anyone in the eye or began to speak, it would all be over. I could not keep up the facade. The pressure was too much, and I was cracking! My hands shook. My head was pounding. I could not eat, and keeping down the pop I sipped on was a chore. I wrestled with the questions in my mind for hours. Ruthie was the only person I thought I might be able to trust. I had no idea what would happen if I told her, but I could not take it any longer.

Walking down to Ruthie's office, I felt sick to my stomach. I turned and quickly returned to my office, trying to catch my breath. I wandered back and forth a few times before I was able to finally stop at her office. Buying time, I made some small talk and then asked if I could speak with her—away from the office. She had a few things to finish up but gave me the key to her home and said she would meet me there. Since I was not feeling well, I left work early and went to her home to wait.

My life would be over soon—I was certain. I planned what to say and just knew she would be angry with me for lying to her and I would probably have to find a new job. So many uncertainties—should I really open this can of worms? But then, how could I go on if I didn't? Again and again, I asked, "Lord, what do I do?"

Ruthie arrived shortly. I had settled into the corner of her sectional sofa. It was the ugliest orange and gold I had ever seen, but it was definitely the most comfortable. After getting some sweats on and grabbing something to drink, she joined me in the living room. The shades were drawn, and there was one dim light on across the room. I was so embarrassed and scared, I did not want her to look at me or see my face.

Slowly I began to share my story. Through a trembling voice, my body shaking uncontrollably at times, and with tears now streaming down my face, I told her how sorry I was for lying to her and asked her to forgive me. Piece by piece, the story came out, and finally arrived at my dilemma of what to do next.

What I did not expect was her response, and I will never forget her tender words. She, too, was crying as she reached out and gave me a big hug.

"You must be hurting so badly. I love you."

"Wait—what? You can't love me." Through sobs I continued, "Don't you realize what we've done? We lied about who we are. We were working with children who you are responsible for. We lied to you, and you say you love me? No! You can't love me!"

"Marilyn, I love you because God loves you!" Her words were gentle and compassionate. She did not have anger or hatred or condemnation toward me.

"But you're not God!"

I didn't understand that kind of love. How could it be? I got up and ran to her kitchen. Crumpling to the floor, I leaned against the oven door as I wept. After a short time, she followed me into the kitchen. She had a cassette player and a song I needed to hear.

The song painted a picture of a life that was broken and filled with pain. Shame and emptiness were abundant with a black cloud of sadness covering the shattered life. My tears continued to flow until the phrase about the picture being "framed with the blackness of sin." That was an exact picture of what my life looked like. It took my breath away as I collapsed again on the floor in a fetal position, sobbing uncontrollably. That was me!

> The artist lifted the canvas
> And sketched each line carefully
> I watched as the picture unfolded
> It was shaped in the image of me
> The shadows were deepened with sorrow
> And the brow was wrinkled with pain
> The eyes were sad and so empty
> A picture of sorrow and shame
>
> He painted a heart that was broken
> Torn and scarred deep within
> Bitter from life's disappointments
> And framed with the blackness of sin[8]

The second verse brought some hope as Jesus picked up the brush and began painting a forgiven heart that is mended.

Ruthie's gracious, loving touch began the healing of my fragmented heart. Her eyes were still teary; she held me as we listened, and I wept. Why wasn't she scared to touch me? How could she hug me now that she knew about my lifestyle? It was as if Jesus Himself was sitting on that kitchen floor, holding me in His arms. I began to calm down a little as I listened to the end of the song.

> I looked in the eyes of the Artist
> I trembled and reached for His hand
> And cried, "Oh, Master Creator,
> Transform me and paint me again."
> So, He smiled and lifted the canvas
> And started all over again
> Remolding and shaping the image
> How graceful, the touch of His hand
>
> He painted a heart that was mended
> Erased all the guilt and the sin
> And framed it with colors of crimson
> I posed and He painted again[9]

After what seemed like hours, I finally ran out of tears, and we made our way back to the sofa. I had a gnawing in my gut—a question I needed to ask, although I was not sure I really wanted an answer.

"What do I do now? How do I fix the mess I've created?"

Again, her words came with sensitivity and love. There was not even a hint of accusation or disapproval. There was no scolding. There was not a list of what I had to do. No should haves or could haves. Just love—a healthy kind of love flowing out and enveloping me in its sweet embrace. I was beginning to taste and experience God's grace like never before.

She said, "I think you know what you need to do."

Nothing was going to be solved immediately. I returned home later that evening, not saying much. I went to bed early, exhausted and needing some rest after that emotional ordeal. What amazed me was Ruthie's unconditional love. She had a confidence in me that I would choose to do the right thing. It had been a long time since anyone had given me that much credit for making the right choice. She did not put a time frame on my sacrifice and bowing in obedience to the Lord. She prayed for me. She somehow understood that God was working and that it would take a little time. She was not in charge of the "when" or the "how" or even the "if." She walked beside me with compassion and chose to love without pressure.

> I was beginning to taste and experience God's grace like never before.

"Okay, Lord, I prayed for You to change me. I'm trying to really listen. Remove the scales and blinders from my eyes to show me what truth is. Lead me because I'm scared, and I don't know what to do. Hold me while I sleep!"

CHAPTER 9

Jesus with Skin On

Early Twenties
Colorado
1986

My early morning, under-the-blanket meetings with Jesus continued. Desperate to be shown what to do, I could not wait to meet with Him each morning to see if He would give me more direction. Over the years, I had allowed other people to make many decisions for me, telling me what I should do. Never before had I made such a big decision on my own, for my own life. I was not sure if I was ready for this since I would be putting all my dependence on the Lord and trusting that He would guide me, but I had to continue taking steps in His direction.

The struggle of figuring out what to do did not last long, although I am unsure how much time passed. God's Word had penetrated my heart, and I knew the answer to my question. I loved Kris, yet I loved Jesus more and wanted to be obedient to Him. Obedience and the choice to follow God were not something forced on me, but as I drew near to His heart, the truth rose to the top. Spending time in God's presence, I was more aware of His holiness as well as my sinfulness. In order to obey, I would have to walk away from the only stability I knew in life.

My marriage (civil union) was never binding in the eyes of God. He designed marriage to be between one biological man and one biological woman. Since I had gone against God's will and what He established from the beginning of time, repenting and turning back to Him and His ways would mean walking away from this union. In God's eyes we were never really married, but in man's eyes there was a legal document, so there would have to be a legal dissolution of the marriage.

> I loved Jesus more and wanted to be obedient to Him.

The process of turning my focus toward Jesus and the next few steps of obedience were extremely daunting. My life on the high seas had calmed for a time, but currently, the storm and waves threatened my very existence as I knew it. It felt as though I would soon endure the unthinkable—getting out of the boat and walking on water. I liked the boat—marriage and the family I was in. I was comfortable where I was—the known vs. all the unknown that lay ahead of me. I was not angry with the boat's captain—Kris had called the shots for quite some time, which was fine by me. However, I was being called to do something I had never done before—trust Jesus with everything I had and

> I was being called to do something I had never done before—trust Jesus with everything I had and step out of my safety and comfort.

step out of my safety and comfort. My focus was on Jesus' face, and He was beckoning me, "Come!"

Since the Lord had clarified the first step of walking away from the homosexual lifestyle, my next question was a matter of when. If my obedience was given the opportunity to delay, I knew it could quickly turn to disobedience again. I had to take the next step, and the sooner, the better. If God was calling me to obedience, I needed to do it right away.

"Lord, You have called me to do something that scares me more than ever. I don't know what to do with my life. I don't know how to take care of myself and make decisions. I don't know how I'll make it financially. But if You want me to obey, then You will have to take care of all those other things, too. Help me, Lord. With Your strength, I can and I will do this!"

~ ~ ~ ~ ~

Jealousy had begun to grow in Kris. He must have sensed that something had changed. I was growing colder in the relationship and indifferent to our future plans, which seemed to be infuriating him. There was not any visible abuse, but Ruthie sensed something was not right. One night after church,

Kris became upset, and I saw them talking outside her office. It was not loud, but there was definitely some drama.

Later that week, Ruthie and I met again at her home after work.

"Ruthie, you know how I felt trapped, like I couldn't divorce because I had been taught God hated that, yet I didn't have peace about moving forward because I was in a homosexual relationship? Well, God showed me what to do, and I am scared to death—but I finally have peace. I am going to walk away from it all. I am choosing to love Jesus more than my partner of six years."

She gave me an affirming smile and said, "I knew you would. I believed in you, kiddo!"

Those simple words were like a stadium full of angels cheering me on. I needed that.

"Now, you have to promise me something. When you tell him, you need to make sure you are out in public somewhere. Kris could get really angry and upset. You need to drive separately and be around a lot of people. Then when you are done, come stay at my place for a couple of nights until he calms down." God had placed Ruthie in my life at this time to help me walk through this difficult situation.

Although confused by her great concern, I was willing to take her advice and assured her I would do as she suggested. "Good job," she said, "and I'm proud of you!"

"Lord, I have been so screwed up in my thinking for so long. I am realizing I tend to follow people who tell me lies. Somehow, Ruthie's encouragement to follow through with this seems true—like I can trust her. Let me know if this is the right thing to do. Help me to do what You are calling me to do. I want to please only You and not anyone else."

I waited a couple of days for the weekend, thinking that after I told Kris, we both would need some time to process my decision and figure out what the next steps would be. Though I remembered Ruthie's warnings, I chose, instead, to set safety aside. The conversation I would have with Kris needed to be a private moment between us and not involve a restaurant full of people. My desire was to share with Kris what God had shown me, not to just communicate a break up of our relationship. I would have to trust the Lord for my safety.

Steak was his favorite meal, so I prepared a great feast. My heart raced like a champion horse as we finished eating. The conversation was at a lull, so I knew this was the time. As I played with my steak knife and the leftovers on my plate, I briefly thought about what Ruthie had said about having people around.

"Okay, Lord, I guess steak with sharp knives was probably not the best choice for dinner. Oh well, here we go. Jesus, protect me because I'm going to get out of this boat tonight, and I need You to help me! I will obey You—no matter what!"

I began the conversation focusing on where we came from and led into where I was headed. Our friendship started within a Christian youth group, praying for each other, studying C.S. Lewis's *Mere Christianity*, having Bible studies, and Kris being a support to me when Julie died. But we both had walked far away from how Jesus would have chosen for us to live. He was calling me back. I wanted a life with Jesus—for Him to be the Captain in control of my life!

89

"Kris, I'm sure you have noticed I have been a little uptight lately, and things have not been the best between us. I'm not angry with you, nor have I stopped loving you. It's just that, after the prayer seminar at church, God has been tugging at my heart. We both know the truth regarding what God says about our relationship, but we have chosen to live according to our rules instead of God's."

Stopping to take a deep breath, I briefly looked up from my plate to see what Kris's reaction was. He did not make eye contact. His face seemed pale and as though he had a sense of what was coming.

"I have fallen in love with Jesus, and He's calling me to obey Him. I have to walk away from this relationship and lifestyle. I love you, and I don't want to hurt you—but I want to obey God more than anything. My prayer is that you, too, will choose to obey God and turn away from all this. I'm so sorry."

Things were much calmer than Ruthie had anticipated. Tears flowed from both of us as I assured him of my love for him—but I loved Jesus more!

It was the hardest thing I had ever done. Kris was my security, my stability, and the only one I had been close to for so long. Obedience is not always doing the easy thing, but I knew it was the right thing.

We agreed to give each other some time to process what my decision would mean for each of us and to discuss it further at the end of the weekend. The wild ride we had been on for the last six years was coming to an end. I was getting off the roller coaster and invited him to exit as well. Although the pain was devastating, my desire was not to hurt him. I did not want to upset the plan now that he was in the middle of the sex change.

My flesh wanted to stay, hold him, and tell him somehow everything was going to work out. But I knew I could not. I had to place him in God's hands to work out whatever He wanted to in Kris's life. My bag was packed, and I left for a couple of sleepless nights on Ruthie's sofa. As I left, I knew it was right—yet my heart was aching, and I cried the whole way to her house.

> Obedience is not always doing the easy thing, but I knew it was the right thing.

"That was right, wasn't it, Lord? You will help him and show him what to do as well, won't You? If You're big enough to do this for me, You're big enough to help Kris through this muddy water. Show him Your love and acceptance the way You showed me. Give him some people who will walk through this with him and love him back to You. Provide the time, the finances, and the mental effort it will take to do this. Wrap Your arms around him and show him the way to You."

We had left the single's ministry and were attending the young married Sunday school class at church, which was taught by a precious older lady who was full of wisdom. Kris went to her and her husband and shared his story. They were willing to walk this long journey with him—God had answered my prayers. Kris decided to let me stay in the house, and he would move in with that couple. I was so thankful for them and their open arms.

~ ~ ~ ~ ~

Walking through the consequences for what I had done would not be easy. But since I knew it was the right thing to do, I was confident that God's strength would somehow get me to the other side of this giant river I had to cross. Soon I would face the pastors where I worked, one of whom had married us and the other who was the senior pastor. Nothing could prepare me for what was ahead. Scared is not the right word. Terrified is even too calm. I braced myself mentally, believing I would be scorned, chastised, and need a new job.

Kris set up the appointment for late in the day. He would go in first and meet with the senior pastor, Jonathan, and the associate pastor, Andy. They were meeting with us separately and had no idea why. I did not want to be there for that initial point of breaking news. Walking in later would be hard enough, but Kris had the hardest part—telling them the truth. I waited in my office, sick to my stomach and feeling like I was choking. Gasping for air, I cried out for God's strength once again.

After what seemed like hours, the senior pastor's secretary called me. They were done with Kris and ready to see me. That was the longest path I had ever walked. Down the hall and up a flight of stairs, each step feeling heavier than the last. At the top was a glass wall that led to the secretary's office with another glass wall into the pastor's office. Once I hit those last couple of steps, she would be able to see me, and there would be no turning back. I had never wanted to run away so badly.

"Lord, You've got this, right? I surrender to Your will, Your way. I'm ready to receive whatever's coming to me. Just hold my hand, Jesus, okay?"

I was scared. I was shaking. I was ashamed. I was embarrassed. I was broken. The best part was that I would not have to explain everything—just offer my deepest apologies. I was so sorry. There was nothing else to say.

Have you ever been in Jesus' presence? Where you feel you can actually reach out and touch Him? Where your sin is laid bare before you and you have nowhere to hide? Where His grace is the only thing that can possibly sustain you? I saw what Jesus looked like that day. I felt His unconditional love and tasted His grace! My pastors awoke that morning, like every morning, with a desire to minister to those God placed in their path. Today, they would be Jesus with skin on. Literally, His hands and His feet.

The love in that room was such a sweet fragrance. Pastor Jonathan met me at the door, and we joined Pastor Andy at a small sitting area by the windows. Pastor Jonathan fought back tears as he spoke. There was a gentleness and grace pouring out from them that I had never expected. The only other time I had experienced that was when I had told Ruthie—and she loved my broken heart. I cannot explain the enormity of their love. It was truly as if Jesus was sitting in that room with us!

I will never forget Pastor Jonathan's words as he began to speak, "Marilyn, as you know, we have met with Kris, and he told us your story." He paused. I could tell it was difficult and very painful for him. After a moment he continued, "We want you to know we love you, and we want to walk through this with you. Please, don't leave the church. Let us be here for you to help you."

What I was hearing was not at all what I had expected. I sat in disbelief. What do you do with that kind of love and grace? I was in shock.

Pastor Andy sat across from me, wiping away tears. He was the one whose office I would go to for a break in my day to get a smile and some inspiration. He was the one we met with for marriage counseling and who had joined us together at the wedding. They were both deeply wounded—stabbed in the heart. Yet they loved me. I did not understand that kind of love. I have never experienced anything quite like Ruthie's and their love.

Pastor Jonathan's words were carefully spoken and so very gentle. "Marilyn, first of all, you need to know that your job is secure. You can continue to work in the office, but we will have to ask you to step back from any ministry-related contact: no more children's ministry, no more leading Bible studies. But you are welcome to stay as long as you wish." I nodded in agreement, not really knowing what to say. He continued, "We would like you to commit to some Christian counseling to assist you with this transition, and we will gladly take care of the cost. We will help you through this—just stay connected to the church."

I was dumbfounded. As we sat there, I felt like I was transported back to Bible times. I was the woman caught in adultery. They offered unmerited grace and unconditional love, encouraging me to "go and leave your life of sin," a chance to start over.[10] It was the same kind of love I had received from

Ruthie. Jesus' love doesn't hurt! Jesus' love does not bite back with condemnation and conditions. Jesus' love does not have a bunch of hoops to jump through to make us acceptable. He just loves us—right where we are.

The tears leaped out of my eyes. There was not even time to well up and begin to flow. It was just at flash-flood stage immediately. I could not believe my ears—my job was secure? "You mean I'm not fired?" I apologized through my tears. My words seemed so empty. How could I find the right words to adequately say how sorry I was for trampling on their hearts? What could I ever do to make up for the pain I had caused? How could they ever trust me again? This was a love I had never experienced. A love just like Jesus!

> Jesus' love doesn't hurt!

I left the office in awe. Still teary, still shaking a bit, but walking with Jesus' arms wrapped around me in an amazing way. I knew He would help me through this. It was the right thing to do. Oh, how I wished it was all over, but I would need to walk through some deep waters before it was all done.

> He just loves us— right where we are.

I agreed to step away from any ministry and took them up on their offer to stay at my job. So much of my life was in turmoil at this point—I could not even begin to think about finding another job. True to their word, they continued to encourage me, paid for counseling, and walked hand in hand with me through the hardest road I had traveled in my life.

"Jesus, You have revealed Yourself to me in a way that I will never forget. You are becoming that 'Best Friend' Ruthie has talked about, and now I'm experiencing first hand. Thank You, Jesus, for loving me enough to send me to this place—to send me to the right people to love me unconditionally, to point me in the right direction, to offer to walk along side me through the journey. You are lifting the canvas of my life and painting me all over again! You are so faithful!"

CHAPTER 10

Obedience at Any Cost

Early Twenties
Colorado
1987

"Well, Lord, what's next? I heard You have a plan for my life. I guess I messed that up, huh? So can You take all this mess and help me? Do You still have a plan when I make a mess? I'm learning to trust You, but I have no clue what I'm doing. Please carry me, Jesus!"

The arrangement of my staying in the home was getting very old very fast. Living in a house I needed to look after, a neglected yard I obviously had no desire to care for, and maintaining renters downstairs for added income—the energy-depleting burden tipped the scale of my ability to handle it all. I had lived on my own right out of high school, but it was in a family friend's basement with little responsibility. Spending so much time with Kris had made that time seem like I was not really on my own. This was the first time I would have to be solely responsible for a house, bills, utilities, car maintenance, etc.—and I feared I would fail miserably. Emotionally, there was a lot going on as I labored, struggling and striving to walk away from a relationship that had been my life for six years. I was committed to making the change, but it was unquestionably the most difficult experience of my life.

One day at work, during our staff lunch gatherings around the large conference table, one of the pastors began inquiring about my schooling. Pastor Burt, the pastor to the senior adults, had the energy of a youth pastor and a heart the size of the Grand Canyon. He said, "Marilyn, tell me about your education."

Timidly, I explained my brief seasons of college attendance, each ending with confusion about my future direction. There were no more questions. There was no discussion. There was not even an inquiry about my desires. He said, "Well, you need to finish your education!" And with that, he rocketed out of his chair, dropping a half-eaten sandwich in his place.

There was a phone in the conference room, and he immediately contacted the local Bible college. Asking for admissions, Pastor Burt gave them some instructions to send him the bill and told me to get up and talk with them on the phone. He was sending me back to school—like, right now! He had hoped I would carry a full load, but I was only able to handle a couple of classes at that time. I was so grateful for his initiative and willingness to launch me back into the classroom. God was working out the details, using Pastor Burt, to prepare me for my next step of obedience.

I loved school and was excited to learn more from the Old and New Testament surveys, in-depth studies of various books in the Bible, and church history. The professors made the Bible come alive and shared the familiar stories in a way I had never heard before. All that studying bridled my mind, forcing me to focus and align my life in a new direction. The experience was amazing, even though life brought with it plenty of highs and lows. My hopes were that God would use the training to help me through to wherever it was I was going. He knew what was on the other side of the river I was crossing, which, at the time, felt wider than the ocean. In those early days after Kris moved out, I often prayed a prayer like this:

> All that studying bridled my mind, forcing me to focus and align my life in a new direction.

"Lord, You parted the waters for Moses and Joshua. You can do it for me too, right? Help me through these tough times of trying to walk in obedience to You. Sometimes it hurts so bad, I can hardly breathe! No matter what happens, I choose to follow Your lead."

After a long day at work and school, I arrived home from class one night tired yet excited from our class discussion. The phone rang not even two minutes after I walked in the door. I knew it was Kris because I still did not have any close friends that would call me, and my family did not know where I was. I had managed to cut all of them off, so they did not even know how to contact me.

Irritated that Kris seemed to be watching the clock, I muttered to myself, "Really?" I was not sure if I should be talking to Kris, but I missed him so badly. I wanted to hear his voice and see how he was doing. Panic gripped my heart as I debated about my level of communication with him while I continued to walk away from the known into the uncertainty of the future. The anguish of losing the relationship battled within at various points of attack. There was no longer anyone home to share my day with, to share dinner with, or to cuddle with. It was a different level of lonely.

I finally decided to answer, "Hello."

"Hi. I wasn't sure you would answer. I just wanted to see how your class went." His voice sounded sad and forsaken.

Trying to talk through my tears, I shared my excitement about what I was learning, yet I did not want to sound too happy that everything was changing and he was not a part of it. Such conflict warred inside. I wanted to tell him to come home and forget the whole thing—but I couldn't. What had I done? Everything I touched seemed to turn into a mess. I was scared to ask how he was doing because I might give in and change my mind about the divorce.

"Well, it's late. I gotta go."

"Yeah. Okay. Can I call you again?"

"Sure, that'd be nice."

What was I thinking? No! I did not need to be talking to him! I needed to keep my mind clear and focused on looking straight ahead. But I missed him and did not want to hurt him any more than I already had.

"Lord, I don't know how to do this. I don't know if I'm strong enough to do this. You're going to have to show me what You want and how to take steps toward You. Don't let me screw this up! Not now. Show me how to take the next step!"

Crying myself to sleep had become the norm, and that night was no different. Thankfully, morning came quickly, and I was eager to see if God had come up with any answers to my cries for help from the previous night. So out to the living room floor and under the blanket I went. As my face hit the floor, God's presence poured over me once again. He was so faithful to be there, waiting for me each morning with a hug from His Word and fresh steps to take for the day. I still did not know how to follow through with all He was pointing out to me in Scripture, but He was patient enough to keep telling me more each day. He did not seem to give up on me. His Words were so encouraging. It was like getting pumped with energy and the strength I needed for one more day.

"Thank You, Jesus! This is exactly what I needed!"

My morning drive to work was about a half hour—on a good day. I found if I played my music really loud and sang even louder, joy filled my heart and empowered me to face the day. Twila Paris's songs ministered to me in such an incredible way that I could feel Jesus riding in the car with me. I was getting to know my new Best Friend! He was renewing my mind with His Word and the truths in those songs. I was learning to speak truth about trusting God and about having victory even before I actually had it or could see what He was doing.[11]

Each morning, the words to various songs would minister deep in my soul. I would often pause the music to talk to Jesus after each one. More than a prayer, my ongoing conversation with Him lasted all day long.

~ ~ ~ ~ ~

Runner, when the road is long
Feel like giving in but you're hanging on
Oh, runner, when the race is won
You will run into His arms[12]

"Lord, so many days I just don't think I can do this. Help me
to hang on to You because You are my only hope. Thank You
that when my life is done, I will run into Your open arms. You
are my Abba (Daddy), and I am thankful that I can crawl up in
Your lap and know I am going to be okay. I love You, Abba."

~ ~ ~ ~ ~

Sometimes my little heart can't understand
What's in Your will, what's in Your plan
So many times I'm tempted to ask You why.
But I could never forget it for long
Lord, what You do could not be wrong
So I believe You even when I must cry

Do I trust You, Lord?
...You can see my heart, You can read my mind
And You got to know, I would rather die
Than to lose my faith in the One I love
Do I trust You, Lord? Do I trust You?

I will trust You Lord, when I don't know why
I will trust You Lord, till the day I die
I will trust You, Lord, when I'm blind with pain,
You were God before, and You'll never change
I will trust You, Lord[13]

> I choose to believe You, even when I cry.

"Lord, I don't understand all You are doing. I don't understand why my life's path took this turn. I don't understand why You allowed me to be molested. I don't understand why Julie had to die. I don't understand why people I trusted would hurt me. All I know for sure is that You love me and You will someday take all this brokenness and use it for Your glory. I can't see it now, but I choose to believe You, even when I cry.

"Trust! You want me to trust You. Jesus, You know that's the hardest thing for me. Why do You pick the hardest things to deal with right now? Probably because I'm going to need to learn this trust in order to take the next steps. Thank You that You understand and know my heart! I choose to trust You—even when life doesn't make sense!"

> I choose to trust You— even when life doesn't make sense!

~ ~ ~ ~ ~

Every heart that is breaking tonight...
He sees you, He knows you
He loves you, Jesus loves you
Every heart that is breaking tonight
Is the heart of a child that He holds in His sight

And, oh, how He longs to hold in His arms
Every heart that is breaking tonight[14]

"Lord, I can't even begin to put into words how hard this is for me to walk away from Kris. My heart is breaking today. But You know that already, don't You? You see my tears! You hear my cries! You know my heart! And You love me right where I am—broken! Hold me extra tight today, Jesus."

> You love me right where I am— broken!

~ ~ ~ ~ ~

Quietly You lead me to an open place
Hold me in the stillness till I see Your face
Waiting in the silence as You speak my name
Rising like an eagle I will fly

Sweet Victory over the enemy
Gentle Power, all I ever needed
Sweet Victory, I take it finally
Strength for running
It was a long time coming
Sweet Victory

In this place I rest in more than I can see
High above the turbulence You carry me
From deep in a full heart I will speak Your name
Rising like an eagle I will fly

I held so tightly to my fear
There were so many sins repeated
But Your love has brought me here
And the Victory is sweet—Victory is sweet[15]

"Yes, Lord, Your love has brought me to this place. Any victory I have is only by Your grace. Thank You for letting me taste Your love and mercy. I'm walking in Your strength! Baby steps to victory! Thank You, Jesus!"

The more I sang and spoke those words, the stronger I became. My confidence was in a mighty God who loved me and still had a plan for my life. I could see Him working, and I was learning to listen to His voice.

~ ~ ~ ~ ~

My friends from the deaf church continued to be a great support to me. Emily was becoming a good friend, but I was still cautious about letting people too close. In the past, she and Mark had opened their home to young women who needed temporary housing. Since I was determined to let Kris have the house, with all its added stress, I decided to see if I could live with Mark and Emily for a while. I sensed I was needing to be around people who loved me and would keep me accountable. But that would mean I would have to be honest and tell them the truth about my past.

"Yes to Your will, Lord."

God paved the way as Mark and Emily accepted me with all my broken pieces, just as Ruthie and my pastors had. There was not much discussion about it. They were more interested in helping me with my current situation and being able to move forward. They took me under their wings and gave me the real stability I needed during that rocky time. I was thankful to not have the house responsibility but to primarily focus on healing and growing in the Lord. I wanted all of Him I could get. My thirsty soul finally found some water in the desert of my life, and I could not get enough.

Mark and Emily were a huge blessing to me, as they opened not only their home but their hearts. Mark always had a fun project going around the house, while Emily's new dishes from the kitchen always smelled so welcoming. They loved me and treated me like family. I was learning to make my own decisions, and they believed in me all along the way. That encouragement was priceless.

My time of intensely studying God's Word at the Bible college gave me a desire to complete my degree. It quickly became apparent that my education would have to be far away from Kris. Living in close proximity was like an alcoholic living next to a bar. It was too easy to find an excuse to stop by and give him a hug. Although I had cut off any sexual intimacy, my heart was torn and still connected in a way that seemed impure and not God's desired path for me. I had to get away from the temptation of falling back into the relationship.

Fear was attempting to jump on my back and take me down. I realized I needed to move on and start a new life in a new place, maybe even a new state—but where? How would I ever be able to move all alone? What would be the next step in my journey of obedience? It was not the first time I prayed a prayer like this, nor would it be the last...

"God, it hurts so bad, but I believe You want me to put some distance between Kris and myself. I don't understand what I am to do or where I am to go, but I will trust You, Lord. Open up the doors for a school out of state. Show me where You want me to attend. Take my fear and give me Your strength and confidence, Lord. I cannot do this without You!"

> I don't understand what I am to do or where I am to go, but I will trust You, Lord.

Since I was working at a Southern Baptist church, I thought I would start looking at some Southern Baptist Universities. Locating several in Texas, I began my search in the Lone Star State. Whether I was fearful or not, my new quest was obedience at any cost. The excitement of a college road trip brought with it a wide array of possibilities. My curiosity for what God was up to was sparked as I anticipated His fire leading me to the next step of this journey.

CHAPTER 11

God's Whispered Message

Early Twenties
Colorado
1987

Making the needed changes to separate from Kris was more overwhelming than I had ever dreamed it would be. Our move to Colorado had been stressful enough, but having to move apart, going through our home, and deciding what would stay and what would go, made my heart break all over again. Besides packing up the house, I was needing to follow through with the divorce. That was not something I ever thought I would go through, but I was anxious to put it behind me as quickly as I could. Filling out the paperwork, which would put an end to the marriage, was an amazingly easy process.

One thing I had not thought about much was what to do about my name. I wondered if I should keep my married, fictitious name or go back to my maiden name. An older, wiser advisor would have been very helpful at that point, but instead, I made a quick decision and chose to keep the new name because I liked the way it sounded. Coming to that conclusion would come back to bite me later in life.

The counseling my pastors had arranged for me was an interesting experience, to say the least. Having never been to a counselor before, I was a little nervous and not sure what to expect. The counselor looked to be in his mid-late seventies and reminded me of the Irish actor Edward Mulhare who played the dapper Devon Miles in the TV show *Knight Rider*. He spoke in a deep, quiet, drawn-out voice, and after our first introductory meeting, he started our next session with something like, "Sooooo what have you been...processing?"

Unsure of what I was supposed to say, I quickly replied, "Not much. What's new with you?" After a couple of sessions, I finally got the hang of things and what I was supposed to do. I had spent so much of my life, especially the last six years, keeping everything inside and covering up my thoughts and feelings that it was difficult to express myself and begin digging into who I really was.

I began looking forward to my weekly meetings with my new elderly friend. This experience of being able to open up and be honest was scary, yet a refreshing freedom was showing signs of sprouting in my soul. I was safe in this environment to examine and explore and make choices to take my life in a different direction. Part of those choices included continuing my education.

At last, the time came for my college road trip. I was nervous about going but had asked God to give me a strong sense of where I was supposed to attend. He had been faithful to guide me already, so I was expectant that He would show me exactly where He wanted me.

There was a well-known preacher by the name of Dr. W. A. Criswell at First Baptist Church, Dallas, who I had heard of and decided my search for God's direction at that time of my life would begin by worshipping in that church. I was anxious to get on the road but had to work most of the day Saturday. If I drove straight through the night, I thought I could still make it in time for the Sunday morning service.

My adrenaline kept me going through the long night's drive. When I finally arrived at my hotel, there was just enough time to call the church for directions, freshen up a bit, and head to downtown Dallas.

The historic church, whose sanctuary was completed in 1891, was absolutely beautiful with its ornate architecture, large pipe organ, and wooden pews; it had that unmistakable smell of an old church. But by that time, I was so tired I could hardly stay awake. All I remember was the comforting smell of that church and the disapproving attitude permeating from the lady beside me. Maybe I was overly sensitive

> The old life has gone, and the new has come.

because of being tired. Nevertheless, I was thankful I could set aside the distraction of her frustration and hear God speak to me through Dr. Criswell's resounding voice. He read from 2 Corinthians 5, but all I heard was verse 17 and God's whispered message.

"Marilyn, you need to be rebaptized. The old life has gone, and the new has come. I am doing a new thing in your life. People may not understand, but you need this to remember the time I cleansed you and breathed life into a brand new you."

"Yes, Lord. I will follow Your direction. Thank You that You have brought death to my old way of living and have breathed new life into me. Thank You that You will never leave me to do life on my own. I am a little nervous that the people in my church might consider my rebaptism as repentance of something I did to cause the divorce. What if they look at me with questioning and accusations? It could be difficult to explain if someone asks me why I'm getting baptized again, but I will trust You, Lord."

Finally, there was a peace that washed over my spirit that I had not experienced in a long time. I may not have known His whole plan, but being rebaptized was one clear step I could take in obedience. It might be a baby step, but at least I was walking.

My thoughts wandered for the remainder of the service...

Years ago, I had believed in Jesus and asked Him into my heart as a child. I knew my eternity was secure in heaven, but when some family members questioned my salvation after hearing about my lifestyle choice, it made me wonder if my decision as a child was real. I had since come to believe that they were not questioning me to be mean but simply wanted to make sure I knew where I stood before a Holy God and where I would spend eternity.

One of the Bible passages some of my family had referred to, 1 Corinthians 6:9–11, says that those who live in sin (or practice sin continually) will not inherit the kingdom of heaven. Knowing that we all sin every day, I had struggled with trying to understand what that meant. While living with Mark and Emily, I remembered spending time searching Bible commentaries to find a deeper meaning of those verses. My understanding of the sin that was spoken of was a habitual lifestyle of sin.

That brought up several other questions. Since I had habitually been in this relationship for the past six years, did that mean I was not saved? How long is "habitually," and is it different for different people? How long would God have allowed me to continue to live in my sin? Did it have more to do with the condition of and potential softening of my heart and less to do with timing? I may not have been able to support all the questions with a theological answer, but nevertheless, I addressed the issue head-on.

What I found was a God who loved me on a personal level and knew my situation and my heart better than I did. He knew what had happened in my life—the molestation and what had led me to the point of living in homosexuality. He knew there was a tenderness in my heart that caused me to secretly seek for truth. He knew exactly how long it would take before I would allow His truth to seep through the crack in my heart and begin to take root. He knew when the end of my "habitually" was. He was patient and continued to draw me to His loving heart, revealing bite-size pieces of truth as I was able to digest them.

> ...my choices were not pleasing and honoring to a Holy God...

The Bible says grace is a gift not to be misused as an opportunity to continue in sin. It was not a matter of staying in my habitual life of sin to see how long I could get away with it. It was more about coming to the point of realizing that my choices were not pleasing and honoring to a Holy God and desiring to walk away because of my love for Him. The timing of God's work in my life was very personal as He met me—right where I was.

After exploring those commentaries, I spent some time before the Lord, asking Him to search my heart and take me back to that time as a child when I first trusted Him. I lingered there for quite some time, waiting patiently and wrestling with the questions of my habitual experience with homosexuality. Had I really meant it when I asked Him into my heart as a child? Had I truly been a believer and just drifted away from the Lord? Where did I stand now?

> He was now asking me, as He asks us all, to take steps to walk in obedience after Him.

God brought some much-needed comfort to my soul and confirmed that I had, indeed, accepted Him as a child. I had wandered from the truth. He was now asking me, as He asks us all, to take steps to walk in obedience after Him. For me, this rebaptism would be a symbol, an altar built to the Lord along my journey.

There was peace in this new life God was calling me to. I was putting the old life behind me, and He was giving me something tangible with which to identify this moment. Baptism is a picture of Jesus' death and resurrection. My old life would be buried, and I, as a new creation, would be raised up out of the water to walk in the newness of life. I did not understand how God could forgive all I had done, love me unconditionally, and look at me as righteous—a new creation. That blew my mind. But I would have to accept it for now and grow in my understanding as I cultivated my love for Him by continuing to study His Word. He would continue to reveal truth to me as I obediently sought after Him. I could hardly wait to get back to Colorado to ask Pastor Jonathan to rebaptize me.

My mind was jolted back to the present as the service ended and everyone began to stand. I praised the Lord for His interruption to my morning in church. Exhausted, I was ready to get some sleep, but first, I needed to get out of downtown Dallas.

I had asked for directions to get to the church but had not imagined it would be so difficult to get out of downtown. There were so many one-way streets, no GPS at that time, nor did I have a map. The mountains that I had grown accustomed to in Colorado to aid my misguided turns were obviously nonexistent in Texas. After circling downtown several times, first up this one-way street and down another one-way street again and again, I pulled over to the side of the road and just cried. I did not like feeling trapped among all those buildings. After a few more attempts, I was able to maneuver my way out of the downtown maze and back to my hotel. Finally, I could sleep, and then, Monday, I would begin the college search to see where I would spend the next chapter of my life.

~ ~ ~ ~ ~

First on the list was Dallas Baptist University. It was a small school, with just over 1,850 students in 1987. The campus occupied prime property, positioned atop a hill covered in breathtakingly beautiful bluebonnets that overlooked a peaceful lake. As I walked down the broken sidewalk to the student center, my hopes began to sink. The old building looked like it was falling apart. Everything creaked as I walked into the building and down the hall. The carpet was worn, stained, and wavy. The tables and chairs in the dimly lit room where students could study were mismatched, and some were even falling apart. The walls were mostly bare except for a couple of posters highlighting the upcoming sporting events.

Down the hall to the right was the office of the administrator for the resident directors. It was there I would soon check in and receive a key to a dorm room where I would be staying for a couple of days while visiting the school. Each step I took felt like I was descending into a dark pit filled with fear. I needed to be strong and persevere, yet in reality, I was nervous and longed for the familiarity of my bedroom at Mark and Emily's.

Entering the office, I found the secretary to be very friendly, and my fears calmed as she answered many of my questions about the school while she gathered all the paperwork and my key. After we reviewed the visitation schedule, she contacted one of the resident directors to give me a tour and help me find my room. I would have a short time to rest before the meetings with academic advisors and the admissions office later in the afternoon.

In that short time of touring the campus and hearing about the school, I was beginning to get an idea of God's leading.

Upon entering the bare, stark white dorm room that I would call home for the next couple of days, I began to weep. I knew this was where God wanted me to attend college—but it sure was not what I had in mind. The school was about to enter a time of transition where new leadership and new facilities would turn it into an absolutely stunning campus, but I was unaware of that at the time.

"God, really? You want me here? Can I at least go see the other schools on my list and just compare a little? It's so ugly here. Can I go somewhere that's a little nicer?"

I imagined He smiled as He gently said, "No. I need you here."

I was learning that obedience was not always easy. It was not always about what I wanted but more about putting my trust and my life in the hands of a loving Heavenly Father who loved me more than I could even understand or imagine. He was my only hope. I knew I could not do anything on my own, so I decided to give Him every decision and every part of me.

"Yes, Lord."

~ ~ ~ ~ ~

Returning to Colorado after the road trip, I was eager to share my discovery with Pastor Jonathan about what God had told me at First Baptist, Dallas. He was thrilled with the news, and the date of my baptism was put on the calendar. It would be on Palm Sunday. I also shared with him God's direction for me to finish my education in Texas, which put my resignation date just a few short months away. I was thankful to be able to share those early steps of obedience with my pastor, who had so clearly shown me a picture of Jesus' love.

When the day of my baptism arrived, I was so energized I could have jumped out of my skin. As far as I knew, the only people from church who were familiar with my situation were Miss Ruthie, Pastor Jonathan, Pastor Andy, and the couple who had taken Kris in for a short time. Other than that, I was not sure if anyone else in the church had been told. The people I worshipped with each week would watch another baptism that day, but they would not fully grasp the significance of this act in my life. At the time, my focus was not on them. What mattered most to me was the grandstand full of angels I could almost feel, who had gathered to watch and rejoice. It was time for a party in heaven because I had turned back to the Lord and was taking the next step of obedience.

The activity of God's hand on my life over the last several months played like a movie in my mind as I walked into the baptismal water. It was so surreal. I never wanted to forget that moment or Pastor Jonathan's words as they were etched onto my soul. The symbolism of baptism and the work God had done in my heart were an amazing picture of His grace. Pastor Jonathan spoke the words I had heard many times as people were baptized, but today they meant everything to me. "Buried with Christ in death—raised to walk in newness of life." Yes! Only a handful of us knew the magnitude of truth those words carried.

"Praise You, God! Thank You for being so patient with me and pursuing my heart! I'm so glad You won! Thank You; even in my brokenness, You make all things beautiful! I can't wait to see what You have planned next!"

Returning to work the next day was a little awkward for me since it was the day the group of volunteers came to help in the office. I was sure most of them had attended Sunday's service. Fear began to make its way into my thoughts. I was very concerned that I would have to explain why I had chosen to be rebaptized. What would they think of me? What would I say? The questions flooded my mind, trying to steal away the incredible joy I had experienced just the day before.

I greeted the volunteers as they arrived; some gave me a hug and said they were happy for me. Others just went about their work for the day. But there was one in the crowd...I remember her name. I remember her face. I remember where we were in the office. She knew almost everyone's business and seemed to like to get the scoop on the latest news. As I walked past her, I sensed it was coming.

> Thank You; even in my brokenness, You make all things beautiful!

"I was glad to see you get baptized yesterday." Her tone was contemptuous. "Well, maybe now you and Kris can get back together again. I'll keep praying for you."

Normally, I would have recognized that as a kind gesture to pray for me, but with my current lack of trust and knowing her reputation, I just wanted to scream. Thankfully, I was able to keep my mouth shut, give a weak smile, and quickly retreat back to my office.

She didn't know I was the one making the tough decision to be obedient and follow Christ. She didn't know her prayers wouldn't fix our marriage. She didn't know how much her words stung my heart. She didn't know what I had gone through. She didn't know—and I couldn't tell her.

"Lord, this journey is going to have a lot of bumps in the road, isn't it? People won't understand when I make decisions to follow You in complete obedience, will they? They didn't understand You either. Help me to keep my eyes on You and not worry about what people around me may think or say. As I told You that day in Dallas at the old church, 'I will trust You, Lord!'"

CHAPTER 12

God Said, "Go!"

Early Twenties

Texas

1987

A message I had heard Ruthie communicate to the kids in the children's ministry, time and time again, was that of leaning on Jesus as a very Best Friend. What she had taught them through Bible stories, I was living out as I learned to trust His character more than the circumstances I could see. He had given me an incredible amount of faith to believe He was working everything out on my behalf, even when life did not make sense. That faith would be put to the test in the coming months, and I would, again and again, see Jesus' faithfulness shining through my difficulties.

> I learned to trust His character more than the circumstances I could see.

The majestic mountains of Colorado had been a fascinating backdrop to my morning drives for the last three years. Although I was ready for a change, the flat land of Texas would take some getting used to. I could hardly believe I was moving to Dallas, much less going back to school. Things I had once lied to my family about continuing my education as I had moved to Colorado, I was finally able to experience with this move. My strength and confidence were more in what the Lord would do rather than in anything I could possibly accomplish. There was a hope and a joy in my spirit that I had not been accustomed to in a long time as I began to dream about a future career and completing my education. As a full-time student this time around, I would go with a determined heart to give it my all and find God's purpose for my life. His redemption plan for me was unfolding before my very eyes as I returned to school. The great adventure ahead of me would be an amazing journey. I was so thankful for the second chance I had been given.

Prior to the fall semester at Dallas Baptist University (DBU), I had an opportunity to join some students for summer work that promised a chance to make some good money, plus it gave me the opportunity to get to know some of the students. After joining them in Dallas, we traveled by caravan to Nashville for orientation at the Southwestern Book Company before heading out to various states to sell books door-to-door. What seemed like a great idea would soon begin to expose where my gift and talent deficits were.

Our group of four was assigned to a small town in Georgia, where each day began with an early morning cold shower, some exercises, and motivational words from our team leader before knocking on doors. The people were nice, but I had trouble right from the start. Understanding the deep southern accent was difficult, and that language barrier was not assisting in my sales. It did not take long to figure out this was not my cup of tea. Encouraging "Mrs. Jones" to purchase something for her family or darling children, who were climbing all over me, did not come easily. I was horrible at sales! The duffle bag of books I carried for ten hours a day while walking around town became heavier each morning. The little amount of money I had was dwindling quickly. Finally, it was time to look at things realistically and call it quits.

There was a large percentage of students who would not make it all summer, and the book company had a plan for dealing with non-salespeople like me. After using all of my money for a bus ticket to get back to the company headquarters in Nashville, they debriefed me and tried to reassure me that I was not destined for the poor house just because I could not sell books well. The company purchased a bus ticket for my return to Colorado, and I was given $20 to go along with my ration of food: a package of saltine crackers. Although I was relieved my book-selling days were behind me, going back to Colorado and potentially running into Kris brought on a bit of anxiety.

Riding across the country on a Greyhound bus was definitely not the quickest way to go, but it afforded me plenty of time to reflect on what I had learned selling (not selling) books. I also spent time contemplating and crying out to God to help me know what my next steps were. Feeling like a failure, I hoped the next few weeks before school would go better than the first few weeks of summer had. Leaning my head against the window and trying to find a comfortable position, I began to think about my parents and the farm. I had never spent much time looking at how much faith it took to be a farmer, burying the seed in the ground and praying it would someday begin to sprout. I was thankful for all they had taught me on the farm through their example, without them ever really knowing they were planting seeds of faith in my heart as well. I pulled out some paper and a pen and began to write their long-awaited letter, telling them of the change God had made in my life and thanking them for their life example to me. It was awkward and hard to begin building that bridge back to family, but I had to try.

After more hours on the bus than I would like to remember, I finally arrived back in Colorado, where Mark and Emily took me in for the duration of my stay. I was able to find some part-time work to get by, but depression set in quickly. Life had been so much easier with Kris. Was leaving town really the best decision? Should I have gone through with the divorce? The enemy jumped on those thoughts quickly and invited all his friends: doubt, insecurity, loneliness, and fear. Mark and Emily reassured me and were very patient with me as I struggled mentally and emotionally through those burdensome days.

Weighing heavy on my mind was my need for transportation to go to work as well as to get back to Dallas in a few weeks. Earlier in the summer, when I was attempting to be a salesperson, I had asked Kris to sell my car because I was unable to keep up with the payments. Most of the money from that sale had been used for rent with a small portion left to live on before leaving for college. Mark and Emily's graciousness to me was incomprehensible at times. While feeling quite overwhelmed with the move and life changes ahead of me, they took me in as family, calmed the present crisis, and allowed me to use one of their vehicles as needed.

One evening, as I drove to church, I was praying about my car situation and asking the Lord to provide exactly what was required to get to Texas. He knew how much money I had and what type of vehicle would hold my belongings. As I prayed specifically about the size, I pulled up to a stop light. My gaze was directed to a corner lot where there was a huge "for sale" sign on a car. It was very large and would work perfectly to hold everything I needed to take with me to school, but it was an old black hearse. I began laughing and realized God was covering me with the peace that He had everything under control. In the midst of uncertainty, His sense of humor in all this was refreshing. He loved me so much and would provide exactly what I needed at the right time.

Driving home from work a few days later, I saw another car for sale—a 1976 Chevy Impala. It was not quite as large as the hearse, but it was still a big boat. The man only wanted $200, and I was so excited—not realizing there was a reason it was so inexpensive. To me, it was God's answer to my prayers. Cheap or not, I was going to trust Him. Little did I know my faith would get a workout with that car! I named it Lazarus for reasons that will become obvious shortly.

God was honoring my steps of obedience and had another blessing for me before leaving the state. A Billy Graham crusade was scheduled to be held in Denver in the middle of the summer. It was close enough for me to attend, and the timing was perfect.

When I arrived to the crusade, the crowd was bigger than I had anticipated. Walking into that grand stadium with all those people ready to hear such a godly man speak truth administered a layer of healing balm to my soul. It would be a sweet send-off to school and the new life God was calling me to.

Having gone alone because I did not want any distractions, I was able to sit back and take it all in. I reflected back on the many crusades I had seen as a child. One of my grandfathers would call us every time Billy Graham was on TV and tell us to turn to the channel televising the event. Grandpa would be thrilled to know I was able to attend a crusade in person.

> I had made up my mind to face each day as an adventure and acknowledge my trust in Jesus.

God had already done so much in my life during the past few months—I could not imagine what more He would have for me. But that experience was incredibly moving, and I was thankful to be there, watching people respond to the Lord, just as I had done recently. My heart was filled to overflowing. God knew I needed that boost of encouragement as I moved to Texas and put my life of homosexuality behind me for good.

~ ~ ~ ~ ~

Walking away from everything familiar in Colorado, I entered a new world of dependence on the Lord. There were so many unknowns ahead of me that I could have allowed to overpower any sense of confidence I had at that point. Determined to continue to move forward, I had made up my mind to face each day as an adventure and acknowledge my trust in Jesus. There was no other way I could handle this move and transition on my own. I knew relying on the Lord was my only chance of making it. If He had really called me to walk away from that relationship, He had to have something better planned for me. His Word told me to believe with childlike faith, and so I did—every step of the way.

> His Word told me to believe with childlike faith, and so I did—every step of the way.

I would need that childlike faith as Lazarus and I headed out for Texas. It had taken me most of the day for all the last-minute preparations, but finally, I was packed and ready to go. I was extremely grateful for Mark and Emily's continued support, and they gave me one more hug before sending me off. There was a mixture of excitement, fear, hope, and wonder. What would this new life bring? What was I going to major in? Where would I live and work after I graduated from college? These and many more questions flooded my mind as I left.

It was evening by the time I was on the road. I had come to enjoy night driving with less traffic and being able to carry on a conversation with Jesus without much distraction. Shortly after reaching the open road, a song played that I was sure I had heard before but never like that night. Learning to desire the refiner's fire was something I was still learning. I was not sure what God had in store, but I wanted His reflection to be seen in me. For that to happen, I knew there would be some refining close to the flame where the impurities could be burned away.[16]

"Lord, I surrender again to Your will. Burn away the dross and purify me. May my life be a reflection of Your love and character. I have so much to learn, but I know You will be patient with me."

I was hopefully expectant for all that was ahead, yet the tears flowed again. After a few minutes, I knew I needed to get some more lively music going, or I would be worn out from crying before I even hit the border. Some oldies but goodies would do the trick and help me through most of the night.

Early the next morning, before the sun began to make its appearance, I decided to stop at an inexpensive motel for some sleep before the last leg of the journey. After a short but much-needed rest, I rolled out of bed, ready to go. Lazarus, on the other hand, had some difficulty getting started. I prayed God would help me get him running, and soon, we were able to limp across the street to the gas station. I filled him up with gas, but he refused to start again. There was a bit of anxiety as I prayed, but I quickly remembered God had called me to this and had provided the car. I chose to rest in Him and place it in His hands.

"Lord, please help! I don't even know where I am, even though You do! You know what is happening here. You told me to go to college, and I spent what I could on this car. You know I need to get to Dallas, and I don't have any extra money to fix

Lazarus. Will You please send someone with jumper cables to help me get on my way? Thank You for meeting my needs!"

God had met so many of my needs already, it made my confidence in Him strong. I did not have any fear that the car would not start again. It was the car He gave me, so I knew He had a plan. And with that, I sat on the curb and waited for God to answer my prayer and send someone. Not just anyone—I needed Superman with jumper cables!

It could not have been more than five minutes when the next customer pulled into the station to get gas. I stood up with confidence in my Abba to provide as I walked over to ask if they could help me. Of course, they had a set of jumper cables in their trunk, and Lazarus was running again in no time. As I thanked them, I shared that I had prayed God would send someone to help me. Soon I was on my way once again, praising the Lord for His help and singing at the top of my lungs.

Each time I needed gas, I would pray before stopping, asking God to direct me to the right gas station where He would also have someone available to assist me with a jump to get me on my way. Over and over again, He was faithful to guide me to where someone with cables was available and willing to help. All I had to do was ask God to meet my specific needs. I was beginning to get an understanding of His love for me and His desire to walk with me through each part of my day.

"Lord, You are amazing. You have provided for me every step of the way, and I am grateful to You for that. I don't know anything about cars, but You do. Please get me to Dallas and onto campus without Lazarus completely dying so I can get to registration in time. I know You will provide someone later to look at Lazarus and know exactly what is needed. Thank You for protecting me and going before me!"

Walking by faith. I had heard about it. I had read the Bible stories. But this was a new experience. It was exciting to see God work and move on my behalf—not because I demanded He do it but because He is God and He could. Everything did not always go the way I had hoped, planned, or even prayed it would, but I knew He had a purpose in it and would work all things out. Trusting was hard, yet I realized I had a peacefulness and a rest I could not explain. I would do what I could, but God was always faithful to do His part as only He could.

~ ~ ~ ~ ~

When I finally made it to campus, I took a long, deep breath and headed over to registration. Ruthie had taught me that sometimes you have to walk in and act like you know what you are doing. By the time they realize you don't, you have hopefully figured it out! I took her advice, stood up tall with my shoulders back, and once again, asked Jesus to hold my hand because I felt like I was walking into unknown territory, and I needed Him to guide me and give me His strength.

Following the signs, I worked my way through the maze of booths handing out campus maps and general information, advertisements for various churches, mission trip brochures, and some restaurants giving out coupons. Several of the clubs, including drama, student educators, and the music department, had booths with their information and lots of candy. Library cards, meal tickets, and parking passes were issued. I was grateful to be nearing the end and for the class advisor who assisted me in putting my schedule together. The line had seemed endless as it wove back and forth through the library's open areas. I was exhausted and ready to be done.

Finally, I could see the end and the last sign, which read "Financial Aid." Already wanting to go empty my car and just get a nap, I pressed on toward the final stop. One more, and registration would be complete. I stepped up to the next available person.

"And how did you plan on paying for this?"

"Well, I don't really know. God just told me to come."

All that "act like you know what you are doing" confidence flew out the window in that instant. The fact that I had absolutely no clue was painfully obvious. She got up to consult with her advisor for a moment, and when she returned to me, I was given someone's name to call on Monday. I would have to meet with the assistant financial aid director to discuss the details, but at that point, I was free to get settled into my dorm room. I was a bit concerned about how all of it would work out but again decided to turn it over to the Lord. There was nothing I could do until the weekend was over, so I might as well enjoy meeting some new friends and getting some much-needed rest.

> I was continually in awe as I saw my circumstances were never too much for God's resources.

God is interested in our details. I met with the person from financial aid, and to my relief, God was directing her steps concerning my account. Each semester there were enough grants, along with a small amount of loan assistance and work-study, to get me through. That continued all the way through the next three years. God made a way when it seemed impossible! He was proving Himself to be faithful in ways I had no control over. I was continually in awe as I saw my circumstances were never too much for God's resources. I walked in full confidence that He would provide; after all, He was the One who had told me to go!

CHAPTER 13

"Prodigal, Go Home!"

Early Twenties
Texas
1987

School was off to a great start. I felt extremely blessed to finally be completing my education. Life had taken on new meaning, and I was notably excited about each day. The bounce in my step was returning, and I was eager to connect with new friends. A handful of students and employees close to my age had a desire to grow spiritually, and their relationships with Jesus were infectious. They would become some of my dearest friends.

While I was moving on with new friends and college in Dallas, Kris's periodic phone calls would draw me back into the memories of what used to be. The conversations were awkward, but I tried to be kind and encourage him the best I could. I was beginning to sense that my contact with him, although sporadic, would soon have to completely end.

Mark and Emily continued to check in from time to time. It puzzled me that they never questioned whether my lifestyle change was authentic. I had spent many years deceiving people in my past, so it was important to me that they knew the decision I had made to walk away from homosexuality was permanent.

> ...they never doubted me and deferred the right to judge to a Holy God.

I wrestled with wanting to verify my new identity before them, yet they never doubted me and deferred the right to judge to a Holy God.

I looked to them as spiritual parents and wanted them to know that my love for the Lord was genuine and that I was growing as a believer. I would be able to sit down and share with them face to face very soon. There was a deaf camp in Oklahoma at the end of October that they were going to that was close enough for me to attend as well. I was so excited and could hardly wait to see them.

Lazarus was feeling better at this point because one of the college guys had looked him over and tweaked a few things for me. I was assured there should not be any problems driving up to deaf camp as long as I stopped every couple of hours to add water to the radiator. My only other concern was rain. I kept extra towels beside me due to the one leak, which just happened to be right over my lap. I would lay a towel across my legs and press on, trying to ignore the constant dripping right in front of my face. This was God's car, and I was thankful for it—leaks and all. I knew He would keep it going as long as I needed.

This trip would be short compared to others I had taken that had covered several states. As I drove, I talked to God and praised Him for His faithfulness to me. I was overjoyed to connect with my spiritual support group early in the school year and so grateful for this opportunity. Something inside me was compelling me to go to this camp. The force drawing me was like a magnet—I just had to be there. Although I was not sure why I had to go, I looked forward to soaking up more Bible teaching and time with friends.

When I arrived, there were the normal transitions of people finding and settling into their cabins. Having been to another deaf camp in Colorado, I anticipated some confusion in the communication for me. They were all moving along smoothly, but I was desperately trying to keep up with conversations, what was happening next, and where I was supposed to go.

I was thoroughly enjoying my time at camp. The sights of people signing and sounds of laughter brought comforting memories of when I connected with new friends at the Colorado deaf church. Those memories continued to dance through my mind as the evening session started on the second night. I found a seat in the back and was soaking it all in, watching the praise flow from their fingertips. The experience of worshipping Jesus with my deaf brothers and sisters took me to the foot of the cross every time. This was not my first language, but I knew enough sign that I could join them in song.

Something was different about tonight. I could not quite put my finger on it, but there was a sense that God was up to something. After a short prayer, we began to sing again, and I started to weep. I wiped tears away over and over, but they continued. I could not explain it, and I could not make them stop. Finally, they slowed as we sat down to hear the message the Lord had for us that night. Little did I know God had orchestrated that night just for me. Before the night was through, He would touch my heart in such a way that I would never be the same again.

The preacher began, "Turn in your Bibles to Luke 15. Tonight we are going to look at God's great love and grace as we read about the prodigal son."

His words turned the faucet on inside me, and the tears began again with a constant drip. No matter what I did, there was no slowing them down. His illustrations and sermon points were nothing new. I had heard this story a hundred times, but this time, the vividness of the prodigal was coming alive.

Even though the story was familiar, I saw myself like never before through this Bible story. I was that prodigal. I had walked away from the Lord and left home. My family had not known where I was for a good part of five years. Now, sitting in the midst of two hundred deaf people, God, again, spoke to me as clearly and gently as I have ever heard Him.

"Marilyn, it's time for you to go home."

"Lord, no, I don't think so! You see, this prodigal's story is wonderful, and I love the way it ends and all, but that's not my story. I could never go home!"

"Marilyn, you need to go home."

"But what if my dad doesn't welcome me the way the father in the story did?"

"It does not matter. I have welcomed you with open arms, and I have forgiven you. Now, go home. It will be okay; I will be with you."

As the message came to a close, there was an urgency to go to the altar to pray. I was not sure what I was supposed to say, but I stepped out of my row and down the aisle with much fear and trembling. There was an open spot on the left side of the stage. I knelt down and bowed my head in submission to my Heavenly Father's tugging—and He began to do something in my heart that could only be explained as God's healing touch.

"Jesus, I don't even know what I'm supposed to pray. I thought I dealt with all this when I was in Colorado. What more do You see in my heart that needs to be addressed? Why did You call me to come to the altar? Whatever You are wanting to do, I fully surrender to Your work. Bring to the surface all the things that I have not yet faced. Don't let me keep anything hidden from You. Search my heart, Lord. You know my thoughts, my ways, my future."

> He gently cut away the areas that hid the slivers of my shame and unforgiveness.

I stopped for a moment and waited on the Holy Spirit. There was a cleansing taking place deep within my heart, though I could not fully recognize all that He was washing away. I felt like I had crawled up on an altar, fully vulnerable before a Holy God, where He could do heart surgery. He needed me to be still as He gently cut away the areas that hid the slivers of my shame and unforgiveness. Sin and twisted lies had wedged themselves into my heart far beneath the surface, and the pain of leaving them there was more severe than coming to the altar. The shame of who I had been, with all the labels that went along with it, weighed heavy on me. As I looked into His eyes, that all seemed to fade away, and the word replacing it was "forgiven."

"Lord, thank You for Your forgiveness and for seeing in me the potential of who I can become. But I'm scared of myself—who I am, what I may do, what I can think and feel. If I was so easily swayed into a lifestyle that I knew was not pleasing to You, then what else am I capable of becoming? Where are the places of vulnerability in my life? Please patch up the holes where the enemy can get in to tempt me. Remove any and all desires to return back to Kris. Remove anything that would make me walk into that kind of relationship again with anyone else. Please protect me and keep me safe from any temptations toward homosexuality. Heal the pain that young man from church inflicted on me. Give me a desire to be married to a man and the ability to trust someday. Change my thinking and give me the mind of Christ. I'm so sorry. Cleanse me, Lord. I am so very sorry."

I had no sense of anyone else in the room. It was just Jesus and me doing business on my heart. There were times when all I could do was just weep. The words would not come, only groaning and sighs that God alone knew what they meant. Others who came to pray over me may not have known exactly what to say, yet God heard the cries for help and a symphony of praise. Periodically, something specific would come to mind that I needed to tell Him.

"Lord, I am so sorry for how I have hurt my family. I can't even imagine the depth of their pain, but You know it. Please renew and restore my relationship with them. I don't know how You could even do that, but I believe You want to. Heal them and help them to be able to forgive me."

I told Him how sorry I was for my choices. I knelt, still in His presence, as Abba poured His grace into every crevice of my being. I wept long and hard, pouring out my deepest fears, my heartfelt apologies, and all of my "what ifs." He washed me white as snow, forgiving my sin and remembering it no more. There was a rushing river of love and mercy flowing over me. I was not about to get up and miss out on any of it. I wanted all He had for me and humbly bowed before the throne to receive and drink in His grace.

"Lord, how could I ever go home? How do I begin to heal the broken relationships with my family? How do I ask for forgiveness? How will they be able to believe and trust me again? Where do I start?"

Each question I asked the Lord was met with His gentle voice.

"I know it is hard, Marilyn! You are going to be fine! You will get through this—just trust Me!"

When I finally lifted my head, the room was nearly empty. God had spoken to me clearly, and I had heard His voice. The Shepherd was leading me home. The tremendous healing at the altar that night was only the beginning. Layers of pain and hurt would take years to work through, but at least I had started the journey.

As I walked back to my cabin, my heart was filled to overflowing. I reflected on what had happened that night. It was time to obey—again. I was beginning to get the idea that this was how my life was going to be. One baby step, a little growth, and then God calling me to take another and another and another. He did not want me to get too comfortable where I was but seemed to be stretching my faith to rely fully on Him and His direction for this journey of obedience.

"Thank You, Lord, for loving me right where I am and for the healing You did tonight. I love You, Jesus. I don't know how You will work out the details for my trip home, but I will obey."

On the way back to Dallas, I stopped by my childhood friend's home. Sharon, the pastor's daughter who had welcomed me into the youth group many years earlier, lived in Oklahoma and was anxious to, once again, welcome me in. I had forgotten that she had received the same "tell-all" letter that I had sent to my siblings several years earlier. She had spent the last five years praying for me and was overjoyed to hear about the change in my life. What a blessing it was to spend some time with her reflecting on how God had answered her prayers.

~ ~ ~ ~ ~

Upon my return to school, something felt different, like I was on a mission. God had done a mighty healing in my life for a purpose, and I wanted to know where He was going with this. There was a prayer room in the basement of the dorm that had become my private prayer closet. Setting aside 10:00 p.m. as often as I could, I would meet with the Lord, just as I had so many times during those early Colorado mornings. I needed to hear His direction.

"Okay, Lord, what's next?"

God was guiding me to completely cut off all communication with Kris. It would be difficult to tell him to stop calling, but I had to. My allegiance was to my Heavenly Father. I loved Him and wanted to obey when He spoke. There were to be no cracks where the enemy could sneak in and open up the relationship with Kris again.

Rather than waiting for Kris to get in touch with me again, I decided to take the initiative and make the call. Waiting until my roommate left, I said a quick prayer and reached for the phone. My heart raced as it had the night I told him about my decision to follow Jesus. I was nervous, but I just wanted it to be over.

"Hey, Kris. How are things going?"

He always seemed glad to hear my voice. The last couple of times that he had called, it also sounded like he was making some positive moves forward in life without me. Tonight, his mood was cheerful, which would make what I had to say a little easier. After a little small talk, I decided to address what I had called about.

"So I am going to have to ask that we not communicate anymore. I've told you before I'm not wanting to hurt you, but I really feel God leading me to totally cut things off."

He was silent. I knew this was not what he was wanting to hear, and there was no easy way to wrap it up. I just needed to finish and hang up.

"I hope things in your life go well. I'll be praying for you, Kris. Good-bye."

As I hung up the phone, I flopped down on my bed. Although I knew I was doing the right thing, and I knew it was time, it still hurt all over again. Crying into my pillow, I prayed God would honor my decision and that He would draw Kris back to Himself.

~ ~ ~ ~ ~

With the Kris chapter of my life now closed, I was ready to face the next assignment of reconnecting with my family. I believed it would be all right in the end, but getting there from where I was would not be an easy task.

"Lord, how on earth will I do this? I haven't been home in more than five years, nor have I spoken to my parents since they came to Colorado to try to rescue me. I am committed to following Your direction, but I really need Your strength for this. Give me a plan and Your words when I speak to them. This is Your idea, so I'm trusting You to lead me."

My parents knew I was divorced and going to school in Dallas, but that was about it. When I had written the letter to them on the bus ride back to Colorado, I had mentioned my plans to complete my education in Dallas. They had heard about me finishing my schooling before, so I would not be surprised if they were skeptical. I was worried about what they would say. What if they would not want to speak to me? What if they did not want me to come home? What if they would not believe that I had changed? I finally realized I could not focus on all the "what ifs" but needed to just do what God had told me to do.

> This is Your idea, so I'm trusting You to lead me.

This was still a very private issue for me. Even though God had done much healing in my life, I carried the concern of contacting my family alone. My best preparation had been spent on my face before the Lord in the dorm basement's prayer room. Now it was a matter of following through with the commitment I had made to Him and making that call. My roommate was gone for the day, so I knew I would not have to worry about her walking in while I was on the phone. I paced back and forth in the small dorm room, trying to get down exactly what I was going to say. Finally, taking a deep breath, I dialed their number.

What seemed like an eternity for someone to answer gave me time to whisper another prayer for God's strength and for Him to give me the words to say. Mom answered, and although she seemed happy to hear my voice, there was a cautiousness on both our parts. We spoke briefly about surface things, and then I spit it out whether I was ready or not.

> I could not focus on all the "what ifs" but needed to just do what God had told me to do.

"I was wondering if it would be all right for me to come home for Christmas. I can get myself up there, but I was hoping to catch a ride back to Dallas with you and Dad on your way to California for the winter."

It was quiet for longer than I had anticipated. I don't think she was expecting to hear that I wanted to come home. She could have been figuring out if there would be room in their car that they would pack for a six-month stay on the West Coast. Whatever the reason for the bit of hesitation, she agreed. I had been holding my breath, waiting for the answer that I had hoped for. Now I could breathe a sigh of relief. We were a long way from healed, but at least it was a step. We were on our way. I understood I would need to be patient as trust was built back up with them. I had lied to them so much over the years, and they needed to see if I could be believed again.

This would be a reconciliation with not only my parents but with my siblings as well. I had planned to travel to each of their homes and spend some time with them individually—to apologize, ask their forgiveness, and begin to repair the relationships. I purchased copies of Evelyn Christenson's *Lord, Change Me!* to give to my parents and siblings. God had used that book so powerfully in my life, and I wanted to share it with each of them.

Calling my siblings was much easier than calling my parents. One after the other, I would give a quick update and ask about their families. They had heard from Mom that I was in Dallas and knew there had been some kind of change in my life. I asked each of them if I could spend a couple of days at their home and if they would then take me to another sibling's home. Each one lived one to two hours down the road from the next, getting me step by step closer to my parent's home. Each sibling graciously welcomed my request and agreed to get me to my next destination.

I could not believe this was actually going to happen and take place the way God had told me. I knew He was faithful, but I questioned sometimes how He could work things out. I looked forward to being with my siblings and their families and finally reaching my childhood home and parents to make amends. I was ready for the next layer of healing to begin.

Greyhound travel was not my favorite, but I found that it gave me time to rest from the semester's final exams and practice what I would say when I finally saw my family for the first time after several years of silence. As I leaned my head against the window, I reflected on the memories of family and recalled special times with each individual. There was some anxiety in seeing them again, but the excitement trumped the uneasiness. That bus could not get there fast enough.

My oldest brother's kids were teens now, and I had missed so much in their lives. A couple of them had read my letter years ago when I had shared my new lifestyle, and I would need to find a way to apologize to them, asking for their forgiveness as well. I did not want it to be a generic apology as a group. I had hurt them individually and needed to make it right with each of them.

Stepping off that bus brought all sorts of emotions at once. I was scared about how the visit would go, yet excited to be with family again. Their forgiveness and acceptance humbled me. I was thankful for this opportunity.

The awkwardness faded quickly with their warm embraces. We talked and laughed as we tried to catch up from the last few years. I was able to have those private moments to apologize to the older kids. They loved me and put it behind us. All too quickly, it was time to move on to the next house.

The second brother's home was a little easier because their children were a little younger. After the kids went to bed, my brother and sister-in-law stayed up to talk. They had chosen to tell their two older boys about my situation, and those sweet boys had prayed over and over for their aunt Marilyn. They prayed at breakfast, at dinner, and at bedtime. My sister-in-law shared, "The boys cried when they heard their prayers had been answered. It was like we were able to see what the angels were doing in heaven. Each time someone turns to the Lord, the angels rejoice." Sweet kids—except for the ice cubes they left in my heated water bed that night! I am thankful they were able to see that God answers prayers.

At each home, the children were younger than the last. In the final two homes, the kids had no idea what had happened but were just excited to see their auntie after so long. The time with my sisters was a sweet refuel to my soul. Baking cookies, sledding in the snow, craft projects, the kids and I painting silly faces on each other with washable markers, and lots of coffee with the adults—all while sharing daily life. The love they showed me was a warm embrace. It was apparent that the past was going to be the past and that we were now moving forward. They made me feel normal again by treating me like their little sister and not like someone who had hurt them and lied to them. Grace poured out again and again.

At each home, I took some time to talk with the adults and apologize. They were all loving and willing to accept me and move on. Another picture of God's amazing grace and unconditional love.

Traveling to Mom and Dad's brought with it a whole different level of apprehension. Although I had experienced acceptance with my siblings, and I knew I would receive the same from my parents, it was scarier than I had anticipated. They had received the majority of the lies and the brunt of my rejection when I had told them to leave town in Colorado. Those wounds seemed deeper to me and would take time to mend.

Once again, all my fears melted away in their welcoming hugs. Tears were always a part of my family's hellos and good-byes, but there was a special joy mixed in with these tears. My sister, who had given me a ride, did not stay long. She knew this was a special time I needed with our parents.

We reminisced as we walked through the house looking at new craft projects, wood carvings, and family photos. It brought to mind many memories as well as made me aware of things I had missed out on with family. They enjoyed telling stories about their experiences on the farm and caught me up with the hometown news.

As we sat to have a cup of coffee, I was able to ask forgiveness and thank them for allowing me to come home. They acknowledged my heartfelt apology, and that was the end of it. Their love and forgiveness were more of a private thing for them but fully granted, nonetheless.

Christmas was the sweetest time together with family. I gave them the Lord, Change Me! book and sifted through my childhood boxes to find all sorts of crazy gifts for my nieces and nephews, most of which were treasures their parents had once given to me from their junk drawers. I was so full of joy and thankfulness for what God had done in giving me this time to be home.

"Thank You, Jesus, for this opportunity to reconcile with my family. Thank You for their love and acceptance. Thank You that You love me and accept me just as I am, with all my flaws."

I learned another lesson during that Christmas trip experience. Obedience is not always easy, but it is rewarding in the end. What an unbelievable gift of time with family was given to me as I obeyed what God had asked me to do.

It would take time to rebuild our relationship, but we were well on our way. My parents dropped me off in Dallas and were able to see where I was going to school. I was a little nervous as they met a couple of my friends because I wanted them to believe in me and never again wonder if I was falling back into sin. I was going to do all I could to make sure I never betrayed their trust again. The prodigal was home!

CHAPTER 14

"Yes, Lord, I Will Follow!"

Mid-Twenties

Texas

1987–1990

My Protector. My Provider. My Savior. My Best Friend. I was learning what these words meant as I trusted Jesus in ways I never thought possible. Stepping out into new arenas of experience: returning to school, living in a different part of the country, walking in a fresh direction for my life...sometimes it was a bit overwhelming.

Launched into this adventure of enormous growth, I was so hungry to learn all I could as I talked with God and strived to hear His direction for my every step. Some of that direction came through time spent in the dorm prayer room; some came through listening to preachers on the radio; still, more came from watching the Trinity Broadcasting Network (TBN). Hearing the stories of faith from many who shared how

God was moving in their lives was a challenge for me to keep trusting Him in my life.

As I continued to grow by leaps and bounds, God amplified my faith through cars and driving back and forth from Dallas to Fort Worth for work and church. Lazarus had been named appropriately, as he would often stall out and come back to life just in the nick of time. God protected me over and over again from what could have been horrible accidents. The radiator was leaking, but I could keep him running as long as I filled it often with water. That seemed easy enough. Then, a tire would blow on the freeway, then he would stall right in the middle of an intersection, and then something else would go wrong...I did not have the money to get a new car or to get Lazarus totally overhauled, so I would just pray for protection and continue on my way.

One night on the way to Fort Worth for church, Lazarus began acting a little strange. The gas gauge did not work, but I knew there was enough gas. The radiator had been temporarily repaired, so I was not sure what it might be this time. As the engine started sputtering and stalling, I managed to get over to the side of the freeway and a few yards down an exit. It was getting dark and nearing the end of rush hour, although there was still a large amount of traffic on the road.

The particular exit where I pulled off was not populated, but I could see a gas station in the distance. Between me and the lights of the station, there were a couple of swampy-looking lakes that had overgrown trees and bushes that were not inviting in the least. I had been told it was one of the places police would look for missing people. Definitely not my first choice for a rest stop.

"Lord, now what do I do? I guess I shouldn't have tried to make it tonight. Please surround me with Your angels for protection and send a safe person to pick me up and get me to that gas station."

I thought through my options and a plan to defend myself. Staying in my car did not seem like the best alternative, given the lack of safety of the area, so I would have to take the initiative to get help. With one last prayer for protection and my confidence in the Lord to provide, I got out of my car and began walking with my head held high—and checking behind me every few steps. Making my way further down the exit as quickly as I could, I was also keenly aware of any approaching cars. I sang praise songs in an attempt to ease the fear, and I thanked the Lord for whomever He would send to help me.

Within a short time, a nice-looking car pulled over. My heart was beating fast, and I was nervous as I approached the vehicle. I could not tell if reviewing my safety plan at that point was helping me or increasing my concern. Getting a little closer, I saw it was an elderly woman, and a huge relief came over me. I asked if I could get a ride to the gas station and crawled into her car.

The scene was right out of a Hallmark movie, as God sent me an angel that night named Annabelle Baumgardner. She seemed somewhat distraught as I got in.

"I don't know why I'm doing this. I don't normally pick up people. I just don't know why I stopped."

I smiled and said, "I do. I prayed God would send someone safe to give me a ride. I'm so thankful He sent you!"

With that, she relaxed a bit as we headed toward the gas station. I had told her I was on my way to church when my car broke down. Among the comments exchanged, I also shared that I was a student at Dallas Baptist University. Then I inquired about where she was headed for the evening. For some reason, she was not too sure about sharing what was on her agenda for the night.

"I can't tell you where I'm going." She glanced at me and then leaned over a little closer toward me. In a whisper, she said, "I'm going to play bingo."

Apparently, she had run into Baptists who had condemned her bingo playing. As I got out of her car at the gas station, I assured her that it was okay.

"Thank you so much, and I hope you win a lot tonight!"

A friend from school was able to pick me up that night, and in a few days, Lazarus was raised to life once again. Several times, something would happen with Lazarus that normally could have been very dangerous, but God would always step in and take care of me.

"Lord, help me!" became my prayer of choice!

It was time to ask God to provide a different car. I had learned the importance of praying specific prayers, so I thought about what I might want. Leaving the make and model up to Him, I began my list: gray with cloth interior, four doors, and big enough to pile in a bunch of children; a passenger-side mirror would be nice...I mainly wanted it to run well and get me to school and work for as long as God had me there. He knew exactly what was needed. He also knew how much longer Lazarus would last. So I left it in His hands, praying my specific list often and thanking Him for providing.

I had been working with the children's ministry at a church in Fort Worth for a few months. One Wednesday night, the kids and I were upstairs in a large classroom. We were just getting started with the evening, and as I introduced the night's topic, another worker came in and told all the kids to follow her. Our pastor had told everyone to meet in the courtyard, kids included.

I did not realize what was going on but followed the kids outside as we were instructed. All the people from prayer meeting were gathered out there as well. Pastor Hill was on the sidewalk between the grass and the parking lot. Once everyone was somewhat settled, he asked me to come up to the front with him. Shocked, I went tentatively and stood beside him.

"Marilyn has been working with our children's ministry for a few months now, and we're grateful for her service. But Marilyn, you drive the ugliest car in town!"

"That's God's car, pastor. You better not talk about Lazarus that way!"

The people laughed as he continued. "I'd like you to give me your car."

"All right, it's yours."

"No, I mean give me the keys."

Without hesitating, I pulled my keys from my pocket, took the car keys off the ring, and placed them in his hand. As I did, he handed me an envelope with my name on it. I opened it and began to read it out loud to everyone. Some of the people of the church had gone together to purchase a car for me. Inside the card was a set of keys to my new (used) car. It was gray, with cloth interior, four doors, and a passenger side mirror. I was ecstatic! I opened the car, and all the children piled in. They climbed over the seats and checked out every button for me. My spirit was once again filled to overflowing.

"Thank You, Jesus! You are my amazing Provider!"

That night on the drive home, I reflected on God's abundant goodness and thanked Him...

"Lord, I will name this car 'Barnabas,' which means 'son of encouragement.' You have encouraged me and cared about all the different parts of my life. You have taken me to places I have never been to teach me things I could never learn any other way. My dependence is on You, Lord, for my safety. You have provided transportation for me and taught me to depend on You over and over again. You have taught me to trust Your perfect timing and to ask specifically for my needs. You provide more than I could ever dream!

> You have taken me to places I have never been to teach me things I could never learn any other way.

"Thank You, Jesus, for Your great love for me! You not only love me but care for me in ways that I could never imagine. Thank You for Your gift of the car. Thank You for the loving, giving people of this church. Thank You for opportunities to learn about depending on You in tangible ways. You are so faithful! I dedicate this car to You for however long You want to keep it running. I place my future in Your hands. Use me for Your honor and glory!"

~ ~ ~ ~ ~

Like many students, my major changed a few times throughout my college career. The initial degree plan in elementary education would come to serve as a minor for me as God's plan came into focus. I gravitated to biblical studies and religious education classes as my interest grew in those areas. Having served on staff in the children's ministry, I was intent on learning all I could in that field of study. DBU offered a couple of classes specifically for children's ministry, and I was excited to explore them further.

I loved the ministry classes. The homework was more enjoyable than work, and I could not get enough. One night while reading for class, there was an overwhelming sense of God's presence in the room with me. Then He spoke as I had heard Him before.

"Marilyn, this is what I am calling you to do. You have asked Me for direction. Here is the first step. Will you follow Me into full-time ministry, wherever I lead?"

Was I hearing Him clearly? I knew this was definitely the Lord speaking, but He wanted me? In full-time ministry? Tears welled up in my eyes as the realization of what He was asking began to sink in.

"Lord, this is a huge step—something I normally would discuss with someone. But this isn't something that I can think about or that I can consult my friends about, is it? This is something I either choose to obey or disobey, right?"

I could not even think of disobeying Him, but could this be for real? Why on earth would God call me? After all I had done? After all the deceit and lies? Who was I to be used in full-time ministry?

"Lord, I cannot say no. I am in awe and overwhelmed at Your desire to use me. How could You ask that of me? What do You want me to do? Why would You want to use me?"

Needless to say, my homework did not get finished that night. I turned on some praise music and lay there just taking it all in. As I basked in His presence, questions continued to swirl in my head. *God wants to use me? To serve Him? He is not ashamed of me? He trusts me to do this?* Once again, the enormity of His unconditional love and amazing grace flooded over me. I wanted to shout with joy. I wanted to dance. I wanted to run and tell everyone. I wanted to learn all I could. I did not want to let Him down!

> May I learn to love the dreams You have for my life! Yes, Lord. Yes!

"Thank You, Jesus, for loving me so much that You would trust me to share Your good news with others! Take me one step at a time, and show me what I am to do! I will follow You wherever You lead! I surrender my life to You, Lord! Use me for Your honor and glory! May I learn to love the dreams You have for my life! Yes, Lord. Yes! I will follow!"

UNTWISTING

TWISTED

TRUTH

CHAPTER 15

What Is Truth?

As I prepared for the writing of this book, I spent quite a bit of time perusing bookstores, both brick and mortar as well as online, searching for something that would have caught my attention many years ago when I was still in the midst of my lesbian relationship. At first, I picked up a few works that were supportive of all things LGBTQ. Although I was writing a book about my experience in that lifestyle, that was not what I felt led to spend my time researching. Next, I sought stories of people who had once lived a life as an LGBTQ. At that time, there were not as many as are currently available, but I read what I could find. Their stories were intriguing to me, with some similarities to mine sprinkled throughout the pages.

Still unsure of exactly what it was I was looking for, I scanned the shelves for Christian authors who were writing about same-sex marriage, gay pride, homosexuality, and the church...again, at the time of my research, there was not an extensive selection as there is now. Several of the writings I found then seemed rather angry in their approach. As I read bits and pieces of various books, I thought about how these words would have come across to me back in my prodigal days, and I prayed.

"Lord, this is not what would have drawn me to You. If these authors are what Your church is reading to learn about how to approach the LGBTQ next door, I fear we, as Christ-followers, are pushing more people away from You than we are loving them into Your kingdom. Jesus, I understand having a righteous anger toward the agenda of the LGBTQ movement. I agree that we need to stand firm on protecting the truths of Your Word. But help us to recognize the true enemy and be committed to pushing back the darkness through much prayer and becoming a conduit of Your love to those with whom we disagree."

There were, however, a handful of books I found that seemed to share a story of truth delivered with grace. That was it! That was how I wanted to tell my story—God's love story in my life.

~ ~ ~ ~ ~

I enter into this transition of the book with deep compassion. People have assorted beliefs and approach the LGBTQ topic from a variety of angles based on upbringing, past experience, current situations, and their worldview. Since I am writing to a wide audience, we (the reader and I) may see various aspects of the topic differently. But I believe there is a baseline of solid truth that we can build upon no matter where we currently stand on the spectrum.

Parents and family members who desire change for your LGBTQ loved one, I pray you will find seeds of hope to plant in the soil of a fractured relationship. I empathize with those of you in painful situations and rejoice with others whose relationship with your child has weathered the storm.

Church and ministry leaders seeking to reach out to the LGBTQ in a loving manner while remaining firm in your beliefs, I pray fear and political correctness would never get in the way of ministry. There may be a fine line to walk, but loving them like Jesus while staying true to God's Word is always the right way.

Finding the correct words to express my heartfelt care and concern for the LGBTQ is difficult. Whether you are considering entering into the lifestyle of the LGBTQ, currently living that lifestyle, or possibly desiring to walk away from it, I pray you will read with an open mind and hear my desire to connect with you. You may be struggling to understand where you fit in because the thoughts inside are confusing, but you can know this for sure: You are loved! In fact, you are loved so much by God that He desires for you to hear the truth from His Word. Search it out for yourselves. Ask Him to meet you and show you what He wants to speak into your life. He is crazy about you and will answer your cries for help if you ask with a willingness to really hear what He has to say. His promises are reliable. He says, "Call to Me and I will answer you and tell you great and unsearchable things you do not know."[17] You can be honest with God. He already knows your thoughts, but tell Him how you feel anyway. Let Him help you sift through the lies to find the nuggets of truth. Take the time to wrestle with where you stand before a Holy God. Loved? Absolutely! Can you stay where you are? None of us can! We are all called to continually take steps of growth toward Jesus. So whether you choose to take baby steps or huge leaps, let the journey begin today!

~ ~ ~ ~ ~

You have had the opportunity to peek inside my heart and mind to find out what led me into and out of the homosexual lifestyle. Unlike some, I did not have that early sense of being born with homosexual tendencies. Unlike others, I do not have those tendencies now. But they were very real and very strong at one time in my life. God has taken same-sex attraction away from me, but it may not go away for everyone. God can bring healing, although there may still be struggles and temptations to fight. There is no magic formula or right fix. There is only Jesus for each one of us, right where we are, taking steps toward Him and being obedient to His Word—the *truth*!

> There is only Jesus for each one of us, right where we are, taking steps toward Him and being obedient to His Word— the *truth*!

All of our LGBTQ stories are different. Whether it was abuse, experimentation, rebellion, or same-sex attraction—something led to that arena. Although each one is unique, there are threads of similar colors in our stories, but one thing is universally the same...truth has been twisted. Being a Christ-follower and experiencing the deep impact God's Word made in my life, I present this topic of truth through the lens of His Word, the Bible. But before we consider truth from God, the Creator's viewpoint, we will look at what man has to say about truth.

~ ~ ~ ~ ~

<u>*Dictionary-Defined Truth*</u>

In a day when information is coming at us from every direction, many times faster than we can take it all in, it is hard to know what is true. We hear news and need to consider the source to determine if it is fake. We read stories and have to check the facts. We see advertising and wonder about the fine print loopholes. There is a question man has asked over and over throughout the ages, and we continue to ask today, "What is truth?"

Not only are we asking this with reference to those things around us, but if we stop long enough to ponder, there is also an inner questioning regarding the truth about our existence and purpose. What are we here for? What am I supposed to do? What is life all about? What happens when life is over? There is a hunger to know truth and if what we believe, what we stand on, is solid.

While contemplating a news story a few years ago that highlighted the LGBTQ, I heard a phrase that has been used over and over: "Love wins." Listening to the story that was being reported, I understood what they were trying to say, and it struck me that they were right. Love really does win. Many fighting against the LGBTQ movement stood up and argued their case, but the fact remained: there was truth at the root of their statement, although each side's perspective was different.

Researching more of their slogans, I began to see a pattern of truth hidden inside several of the statements. Could it be that while we, as Christ-followers, are trying to fight the battle against what is being said—their statements are actually true (albeit with a little twist, thus making it untrue)?

This impressed me to mull over truth once again and seek out an accurate definition. Interestingly, the definitions of truth appeared to have been modified over the years. Listed below are a few of Webster's definitions. Note the year each was published and the alterations in the meanings.

Webster's American Dictionary of the English Language (1828):[18]

1. Conformity to fact or reality; exact accordance with that which is, or has been, or shall be
2. True state of facts or things
3. Conformity of words to thoughts, which is called moral truth
4. Veracity; purity from falsehood; practice of speaking truth
5. Correct opinion
6. Fidelity; constancy
7. Honesty; virtue
8. Exactness; conformity to rule
9. Real fact of just principle; real state of things
10. Sincerity
11. The truth of God, is His veracity and faithfulness
12. Jesus Christ is called the truth
13. It is sometimes used by way of concession

Webster's Dictionary (1913):[19]

1. The quality or being true as: (a) Conformity to fact or reality. (b) Conformity to rule, exactness. (c) Fidelity; constancy; steadfastness; faithfulness
2. That which is true or certain concerning any matter or subject
3. A true thing; a verified fact
4. Righteousness, true religion

Merriam-Webster Word Central Student Dictionary (2007)[20] **(italics added by author):**

1. The quality or state of being true
2. A true or *accepted* statement
3. The body of real events or facts
4. *Agreement with* fact or reality

Merriam-Webster Advanced Learner's English Dictionary (2008)[21] **(italics added by author):**

1. The real facts about something
2. The quality or state of being true
3. A statement or idea that is true or *accepted as true*

Webster's New World College Dictionary, Fifth Ed.

(2014)[22]
(italics added by author):

1. The quality or state of being true
2. That which is true, statement
3. An established or verified fact, principle
4. *A particular belief or teaching regarded by the speaker as the true one*

Oxford's word of the year for 2016 was "post-truth."[23]

Truth, by man's definition, has shifted over time. The older dictionary entries state more of an absolute, a fact, or reality of being true. As time went on, the definition included a "statement or idea that is accepted as true." Does that mean there can be a redefining and shared understanding of what truth is? I do not know the intention of the change, but a question of doubt and uncertainty was added to the mix when the definition of truth could be watered down to something we agree upon to be true. It can be corrupted and tainted by man's fluctuating emotions, thus leading us to "post-truth," where everything can be fluid and subject to change. So where does that leave us? Man's definition of what truth is sounds like a rather unstable foundation on which to build our lives and a belief system.

> Truth, by man's definition, has shifted over time.

~ ~ ~ ~ ~

Scripture-Defined Truth

The Bible's definition of truth made its way into the early publications of *Webster's* dictionaries. It was a different day and time back then, but if the Bible's explanation of truth was once there and removed, it is worth taking time to look at it again.

Step back with me to our question of, "What is truth?" The Bible describes truth directly from God's words (as seen in the list below) as well as defines it through the epistles. "For [the apostle] John, truth is ultimately identified with, and is personified in the person of, Jesus Christ."[24] "For [the apostle] Paul, truth is the message of God that all of humanity has repressed and exchanged for a lie, in that they have directed their worship not to the Creator, but to the creation."[25]

God's Word speaks clearly of what truth is, and although many years have passed since its writing, it has remained the same, unchanged. That brings security and comfort to know it will not be altered, but it will stand the test of time. Here are some of those verses about truth from the Bible.

- "All [God's] words are true" (Psalm 119:160a, NIV).
- "I, the LORD, speak the truth; I declare what is right" (Isaiah 45:19b, NIV).
- "Grace and truth came through Jesus Christ" (John 1:17, NIV).
- "Jesus answered, 'I am the way and the truth and the life. No one comes to the Father except through Me'" (John 14:6, NIV).

- "Then you will know the truth, and the truth will set you free" (John 8:32, NIV).
- "Jesus answered...'for this reason I was born, and for this I came into the world, to testify to the truth. Everyone on the side of truth listens to Me'" (John 18:37, NIV).

If we claim to have fellowship with Him yet walk in the darkness, we lie and do not live by the truth. But if we walk in the light, as He is in the light, we have fellowship with one another, and the blood of Jesus, his Son, purifies us from all sin. If we claim to be without sin, we deceive ourselves and the truth is not in us.

1 John 1:6–8 (NIV)

~ ~ ~ ~ ~

> **Jesus Christ is the same yesterday and today and forever. He never changes, and His Word never transforms to something different.**

"Jesus Christ is the same yesterday and today and forever."[26] He never changes, and His Word never transforms to something different. He is Solid. Firm. Set in Stone. Steady. Unbroken. Dependable. Reliable. Pure. Real. Trustworthy. Sound. Upright. Valid. Precise. Authentic. Concrete. Correct. Exact. Factual. Faithful. Genuine. Just. Specific. Systematic. Unmistakable.

Everything I believe is based on the inerrant (incapable of being wrong), infallible (absolutely trustworthy or sure)[27] Word of God. I am not a scholar, but I have read about and studied the works of those who have done extensive research and proven the accuracy of the Bible.[28] Whether you accept the Bible as truth or whatever is essential to your basic ideologies for life and death, we all are trusting in something and relying on a belief system. It is important

> ...will that which you believe in and are relying on...stand the test of time for all of eternity?

to know what you believe and why. The bigger question is, will that which you believe in and are relying on...stand the test of time for all of eternity?

As you have read, in my healing process, I decided to test God, to take Him at His Word and see if it worked. Would He be faithful to meet me where I was? Would He speak to me? Would He protect me? Would He provide for me? Yes! Yes! Yes! And yes! He is completely faithful and trustworthy. Every word of the Bible is true. When I pray, I do not always get what I want, and things may not always go my way. I do not fully understand all His ways, but as He reveals Himself and His direction for my life through His Word, I have learned I can trust Him and His character, no matter what!

~ ~ ~ ~ ~

Twisted Truth

From the beginning of time, the true enemy, Satan, has attempted to twist the truth—to get us to believe half-truths— to put enough questioning in the mix that we doubt what we believe to start with. In the Garden of Eden, Satan presented humans with the option of choosing their way versus God's way, but the choice was never actually his to give. God made us. He is the Creator who knows how life would work best, but unfortunately man chose his way over God's.

If I speak truth and put a little spin on it, is it still considered true? What if I speak truth but leave out specific parts that could alter your view of what I said? Is that still true? Some might say, technically, yes. But when we are answering to authority, it is not a game of how little information I change or how much I leave out and still feel like I am telling the truth. Does that work with parental authority? How about with the police and the authority they carry? What about at our place of work? How much greater is God's authority? Whether it is His Word, workplace rules, governing civil rules, or parental rules, they are given for us to live in peace and know where the boundaries are.

As any of those rules get twisted with a half-truth, partial truth, or even when changed just a little bit, disorientation enters the scene. God's Word draws a line in the sand and says, "Here is the boundary. Do not deviate from the truth." But the enemy's goal is to bring confusion and entice us to step over the line, maybe to step on the line, or maybe to just touch the line with our big toe.

~ ~ ~ ~ ~

Untwisting Twisted Truth

God's Word is *truth*. He cannot lie.[29] Therefore, anything that deviates from the truth is beginning to twist and is, thus, a lie. The definition of a lie is: "a false statement made with deliberate intent to deceive; an intentional untruth; something intended to convey a false impression; to speak falsely or utter untruth knowingly, as with intent to deceive."[30] We must acknowledge and expose the lies. As we identify

> Jesus will meet us in the complexity of our situations...

them for what they are, God can begin a work within us as we learn to walk in the light of His Word.

In the next few chapters, we will look at a few of the LGBTQ slogans and a couple of beliefs hidden within the body of Christ and identify the twist that has been placed on truth in each case. As we do, I realize the wide array of variables in people's lives makes it difficult to communicate with one simple answer. It is not simple. Nor should it be looked at as simple. But Jesus will meet us in the complexity of our situations, and whether you are on your way toward Jesus or not, I pray you will take the next step and join in the journey with a stable source of truth.

When God first put it on my heart to write this, His message was, "Tell them that I love them." With the potential of a wide variety of people with different backgrounds reading this book, I do not want to assume that everyone already knows Jesus and has a relationship with Him. The four LGBTQ slogans I have chosen to address connect to the message of God's love. If you already know Jesus, pray for those reading this who may be hearing about His love for the first time. If you have not met Jesus yet, you will be given an opportunity if you would like to begin a loving relationship with Him and step into the greatest adventure of your life!

CHAPTER 16

Our Nature, "I Was Born This Way"

They had it all. Life was beautiful in the garden. Peace. Contentment. Rest. The food was exquisite. Adam and Eve walked hand in hand and spoke with the God of the universe—the Creator who actually breathed life into them. Their fellowship with Him was on an intimate level of sharing not only their time and conversation but their souls. Who could ask for anything more? What a gift!

But there was a boundary. A tree—the Tree of Knowledge of Good and Evil—whose fruit was off limits. They were free to roam and play and explore and eat of anything else in the garden. Freedom—within limits. Boundaries—for their own good. Protection—only a parent would fully understand.

The animals were gentle and amazing creatures. Adam and Eve watched and interacted with them for hours, but Eve was drawn to one in particular with brilliant colors. Something was different about it. She was mesmerized by the serpent's movements and captivated by its speech. Intrigued, she got up to see where it went one day, not realizing it was headed straight for the center of the garden, toward the tree. Sneaking in and out of view, the serpent made a game of hide and seek that brought her a sense of joy as she searched again for its appearance.

"Come and play," it invited with great enthusiasm.

Play—that sounded innocent enough. Consumed in the little game, she nearly lost her footing as she darted around other plants to find where it went. "Where are you?"

"Up here."

Startled, she laughed. "What are you doing up in that tree?"

"This is the best tree in the garden. Haven't you heard?"

She was caught in its trance for a moment, enjoying their game, and then remembered, "But this is the tree God told Adam was off limits. We have stayed away just to be safe."

"Are you serious? He must be wanting to keep it all to Himself." It cracked the door open for Eve to begin questioning her own judgment.

She relayed God's warning, "He said that if we ate from it, we would die."

The serpent continued the little game of darting in and out of branches. It knew she was moving closer to the snare laid out for her. Just a little closer...it whispered, drawing her in, "Did He really say you would die?"

Its brightly-colored, sleek body wrapped around the fruit, arousing her desire. Its words were enchanting, "Eat. Taste it. See what you have been missing."

Transfixed by the serpent's beauty, she reached for the fruit, confused and detouring from the truth. Maybe it was right.

Maybe one little bite wouldn't make that much difference. Maybe God wouldn't notice. We wouldn't have to tell Him.

Adam was a few steps behind her. He had seen it all take place but said nothing. He saw the look of satisfaction on her face as she handed him the fruit. "The best fruit in the garden?" Nothing happened to her, so maybe he would try a bite for himself and see if what she said was true.

All at once, they knew something was terribly wrong. They wanted to flee—to cover themselves. They must do something to fix this right away. But what? Where could they go? They attempted to make coverings for their bodies out of leaves. God would be coming shortly to stroll with them through the garden for their evening fellowship. "Hurry, let's hide!"

They had chosen their own way and rejected God's way. They were deceived by another and made their own choice to go down the path of deception. Life would never be the same. The knowledge they now had was like nothing they knew before. Good and evil were clear. They had disobeyed God's rule and gone against His authority. This created a chasm in the relationship between them and God. They could no longer live in the perfect garden God had created for them.

Disappointed by their choice, yet still loving them deeply, God had to make them leave. His beautiful creation, made in His image, had not loved Him the same way that He loved them. One day, He would make a way for broken people to return to His Holy presence, but for now, their lives would be changed, very difficult, and separated from the blessings of His companionship.

Adapted from Genesis 2–3

~ ~ ~ ~ ~

The Biblical Truth

Adam and Eve's choice to follow their own way and the consequence of separation from God that it caused has been passed down to every generation. Through Adam's sin, all of mankind is born with a "sin nature."[31] No one is exempt. "There is no one righteous, not even one."[32] We all fall short of God's perfect nature, leaving no one the ability to come into His Holy presence on their own. The Bible says, "For all have sinned and fall short of the glory of God."[33] Even on our best days, we cannot be holy and perfect enough to be in the presence of a Holy God. He wants an intimate relationship with us, to be our best friend, but it is impossible to have a close friendship when there is a barrier of sin between us.

The bad news is, because of our sinful nature, our very being, there is a chasm between God and us for all of eternity. The consequence of the sin nature that Adam passed on to all of us is death and separation from God. When there is a violation of a rule of any kind, a punishment or penalty must be paid. Breaking God's rule or overstepping His boundary is no different. "For the wages of sin is death."[34] That defines the penalty very clearly. The payment we deserve for our sin...is death. There is nothing we can do on our own to tear down that sin barrier and cross the ravine to get to God.

The good news is because of God's great love for mankind, He made a way. The rest of that verse says, "But the gift of God is eternal life through Jesus Christ our Lord."[35] Jesus paid the penalty for us by dying on the cross. He bridged the gap in order to make us justified before a Holy God—declaring us innocent, guiltless, acquitted. We can be free from the guilt and penalty of sin. We can stand pure and holy, our sin payment satisfied, before the Almighty God. When we turn from our own self-reliance in whatever we have placed our hope in, from deeming it "able to save us" for eternity, and instead place our hope and trust in God's plan for salvation, the end result is restored fellowship with Holy God forever.

~ ~ ~ ~ ~

Since the beginning of time, we all are born with a determination to take our own path over God's—to follow our own desires instead of obeying God's rules, to sin. Our fellowship with God is broken, separating us from a close relationship with Him. The once beautiful serpent now entices us through a variety of misguided desires: material items, sexual pleasure, money, pride, and success, to name a few. He continues to lure us to take steps beyond God's boundaries for our lives. We are still mesmerized by sin and drawn in before we realize what is happening.

In light of the fact that we are all born to do things our own way instead of God's way, the statement, "I was born this way" seems to be rather obvious. But what exactly does the LGBTQ person mean when they say this, and where can we find some common ground to begin an open dialogue? The LGBTQ person may be trying to convey that they had feelings from their earliest memories, leading them to be attracted to the same sex—to be gay, bisexual, or transsexual. This may be true.

We cannot determine what they feel, nor can we identify when their feelings began. Yet, we can explore what they mean when they say they were born this way. We must remember their feelings or temptations, in and of themselves, are not sinful.

There are two components to the "born this way" statement. On the one hand, it is very accurate—as stated earlier, we are all born in sin. The confusion comes when we say we are acting in a particular way because of how we were born. At that point, we are, in fact, choosing to act on what we are feeling. Let me explain.

We are all born with a sin nature because of Adam's original sin, but we also have a propensity to lean into certain sins that will push us to cave in to temptation. One may be born with a bent to hurt people through their words or physical abuse; another with a predisposition toward alcoholism or drugs; another with an inclination toward pornography or being a pedophile or a thief or a gossip or a liar. Although a person leans toward various sins, there is a point where we all choose to follow through with that urge and act on the desire. Will we follow God's Word and choose to live within God's boundaries for us, or will we follow our own longings? What do we do with that battle that rages within us?

~ ~ ~ ~ ~

As we look upon God's holiness, learning who He is and about His boundaries through His Word, our sin becomes more apparent. When we acknowledge the sin in our lives, asking His forgiveness, His grace is poured out on us. Once we have been forgiven and justified (made right before God), there is a sanctification process that is ongoing for the rest of our earthly lives. God works in our lives to purify and make us flawless and holy, as Christ is holy. Coupled with that is a progressive surrender of our will, a continual turning from our way (our sins) toward obedience to God's way. Obviously, we will not make the perfect choice every time. We make messes. We fail. But we can ask His forgiveness, get back up, and yield to Him over and over. His love for us does not shrink as we fall down and realize our need to obey once again.

Think of a parent's excitement in watching their toddler begin to take some steps. The wobbliness does not matter. The one step forward and two steps back is still exciting because the little one is up on their feet. They fall, and we pick them up again. They look to us for help, and we grab their hand to assist. God delights in our steps.[36] Wobbly or not. One step or three. We are making strides with Him, yet sometimes we take a step backward. We will make mistakes. But He will always be there to grab our hand and help us again and again. He takes pleasure in our baby steps!

~ ~ ~ ~ ~

Truth and the Twist

Truth

We are all born sinful and choose whether to act on our sinful desires and longings.

Twist on Truth

I was born this way (i.e., with these feelings); therefore,

a. my feelings must be normal, acceptable, and trustworthy, and

b. my actions, resulting from my feelings, are perfectly permissible, allowing me to act in whatever manner seems best at the time.

Combining fluctuating feelings with unbridled behavior brings confusion about what is true. This confusion is one of Satan's greatest tools.

~ ~ ~ ~ ~

> Combining fluctuating feelings with unbridled behavior brings confusion about what is true.

Untwisting Twisted Truth

Our feelings vacillate multiple times every day, drifting like the wind and, at times, blowing with much inconsistency. They cannot be trusted to guide our behavior as to what is acceptable before a Holy God. To base our behavior on our feelings is shifting, dangerous territory. The best navigation to pilot our behavior is to sift these wandering thoughts and feelings through the truth of God's Word. As we read and learn what He has to say, taking steps

> ...the truth of God's Word... will bring stability, security, and safety into our lives.

toward obedience, His truth will bring stability, security, and safety into our lives.

God loves us exactly where we are. He made us. We are His idea—His creation. When we choose to follow our own way instead of God's, His love for us does not diminish. He never gives up on pursuing a restored relationship with us. However, He loves us all too much to allow us to stay where we are, governing our lives by our own feelings and rules.

> ### He never gives up on pursuing a restored relationship with us.

The apostle John speaks lovingly as he addresses his book, 1 John, to "my dear children,"[37] but his love for those he wrote to does not soften the fact that he has some hard things to say.

> If we claim to have fellowship with God yet walk in the darkness, we lie and do not live by the truth. But if we walk in the light, as He is in the light, we have fellowship with one another, and the blood of Jesus, his Son, purifies us from all sin. If we claim to be without sin, we deceive ourselves and the truth is not in us.[38]

John clearly loves them and is therefore concerned about speaking truth into their lives. He cares more about their relationship with God than he does about stepping on their toes.

Moral absolutes have boundaries! There is a line in the sand. God's law and boundaries are meant for our security and good,

> God's law and boundaries are meant for our security and good...

not to hurt us nor to stop our fun. Just as parents give boundaries for safety, God longs for us to stay within the protection of His loving perimeter, which we can find in His Word.

CHAPTER 17

Our Victory, "Love Wins!"

"Why did this day have to come? How could I have been so careless to get caught? Why was I even born?" The thief had just lived through the worst week of his life, culminating with this horrific day. Sure, he had been violent with the farmer's son and fraudulent with his property. There was plenty; he didn't think it would even be missed, and the son had just gotten in the way. But did anyone know why he did it? It didn't matter now. He would not be able to pay the debt and would have to go through with the penalty. Nothing mattered anymore.

"Death!" It was the verdict he dreaded yet deep down had known was coming. He would soon face not only death but death by crucifixion. Like being caught wasn't disgraceful enough. He had seen it before—criminals carrying a cross up to the hill where they would be on display for all to see. Humiliation in death. Why couldn't they have just killed me on the spot? he thought. How long will this agony last? He also knew the extreme anguish that lay ahead of him. Everything seemed hopeless.

Waiting was the hardest part. He had been given the verdict hours ago, but because of some loud commotion outside, they had hurried him to a holding place, hands still tied behind his back. Apparently, there was another trial. He would have to wait until that one finished before they could get on with the crucifixion. There had been a few people at his trial, but it seemed, from all the uproar, that this one was drawing a large crowd. For a moment, he wondered who it was and what he had done, yet his mind could not be distracted for long. Focused on the pain, he knew what he already felt was nothing compared to what was coming. The dread was almost more than he could bear.

Finally, the soldiers came for him and another criminal who had been waiting. The other man was angry and yelled at everyone who came close. Of course, he paid for every careless word with another lash from the soldier's whip. Supposedly, he had stolen gold from the temple and murdered someone in the process. This sentence was fitting for both of their crimes.

They took their place in line as the soldiers whipped them again, telling them to pick up the wooden beams. They each had their own cross to carry, and it would not be an easy task. As some in the crowd were yelling, he heard the name of the third man—Jesus. The name was familiar. He had heard about Jesus preaching to large crowds and healing people. For a second, he thought, *What did He do? How could He be headed to the hill with us?*

The suffering was already more than he had ever imagined. His only hope was that his departure would come quickly, although he knew better. This was meant to be a slow, torturous death.

They finally arrived at the top of the hill where their earthly lives would end. Right before he was shoved to the ground to be nailed to his cross, his eyes momentarily met with Jesus' eyes. They seemed to pierce straight through to his heart, yet they were kind and loving—not at all what he was seeing in the eyes of the crowd. He remembered hearing from others that Jesus said He came to bring life—abundant life. *So why is this happening to Him? We were criminals and deserved to die, but Him?* he wondered. Some in the crowd were calling Him "King." What if He was the true King of the Jews, just like the sign over His head proclaimed?

Time passed slowly. The thief began to slip in and out of consciousness as the pain increased. He had been speculating about Jesus and the possibility of His claim being true. "Jesus, I believe You." He spoke through gasps of air. "I'm sorry for what I've done—the way I've lived." Pausing to get another breath, he said in a raspy voice, "Take me with You to heaven. Please, please, take me with You."

Jesus' head turned slightly toward the thief's direction as He pushed up again on His feet to get some air in His lungs in order to speak. "Today, you will be with Me in paradise."

Jesus' eyes showed unconditional love. His voice did not condemn. When the thief believed in Jesus, a calmness came over him. The physical anguish was becoming more unbearable with each passing minute, but he had an inner peace, knowing when this was over, somehow, he would be with Jesus. He might not understand it all, but he chose to believe.

Adapted from Luke 23:26–43

~ ~ ~ ~ ~

The Biblical Truth

What comes to mind as we approach the topic of love? For some of you, it may be the best thing that has ever happened. For others, there is pain in your heart from a loss. It could be you are still waiting on that perfect one to appear. Or it could represent a deep wound, and you wonder if it will ever mend. Regardless of where love finds you, it is always connected to a relationship, always embraces intense memories, and always touches our lives in profound ways.

> Our greatest victory is not a battle we can even fight.

Sometimes, it feels more like a loss than a win. If we were to scroll through the lyrics of romantic songs, over and over we would see the pendulum of passion swinging back and forth between "you're the best" and "you hurt me." There is such a wide range of emotions to define love. It almost seems impossible to do, yet people try every day through music, poetry, movies, and the media. We long for an adoration that is true and unending. A love that will accept us where we are. One where we can know someone and be fully known. Are these what define a win?

> When other loves fail us, God's love will never fail.

A few years ago, the definition of "Love wins" was all about a court ruling in favor of same-sex marriage. The win is temporal, confined to our earthly lives. But victory is not about just winning the battle for a vote. Our greatest victory is not a battle we can even fight. It is the battle Jesus fought on the cross for you and for me.

Our only hope for victory in the arena of love is God's unfailing love. His devotedness will never end. He meets us where we are and chooses to begin at that point. He fully knows us and is willing to be known. When other loves fail us, God's love will never fail.

God is love, and from that perspective, it does win. The ultimate battle is between God and Satan—the battle between good and evil, the battle between life and death. Love winning on the level of defining marriage may bring short-lived satisfaction, but in light of eternity, it is only a vapor.

~ ~ ~ ~ ~

In the story of the crucifixion, something melted inside the repentant criminal's heart. Jesus' love had penetrated through all the brokenness, through all the sin, and He welcomed the thief with open arms. The sinful man was forgiven and received a free gift that God extends to each one of us today— an opportunity to spend eternity in the presence of a loving Heavenly Father.

But why? Why would He do it? Why would a loving God allow His Son, Jesus, to die that type of death? God saw a sinful, hurting, and shattered mankind that had been separated from His holy presence because of Adam and Eve's choice to sin. His desire was to restore the relationship with us, and the only way was for a perfect sacrifice to pay the penalty for sin. In His sovereignty, God knew Jesus would rise again and conquer death forever, but Jesus still had to walk through the pain of the cross. This would provide a way for those made in His image who choose to follow, to live forever with Him. Jesus' love won on the cross. That is the supreme victory.

The value He placed on us was greater than anything we could ever imagine. "This is how God showed His love among us: He sent His one and only Son into the world that we might live through Him."[39] Because of His holy character, He could not allow sin in His presence. Because of our sin, there had to be a payment. The only payment or sacrifice that would be suitable would be the flawless, sinless Son of God. Jesus was perfect and holy. He chose to willingly give of His life to be the sacrifice for each one of us.

John 3:16 paints a picture of this sacrifice. Let's take a look at it from God's viewpoint. He knows you by name and is a very personal God, so as you read this, put your name in each blank.

"For God so loved_____
"that He gave His one and only Son, [Jesus]."[40]

God loves you so much that even if you were the only person on the earth, He still would have sent His Son to die for you—to pay the penalty for your sin. He gave His Son, Jesus, out of incredible, unconditional love, just for you.

"That if_____ believes in Him..."[41]

Believing is more than intellectually knowing something. It means "to rely on" and "to put your trust in."[42] Jesus is our only hope for tearing down the barrier of sin and bridging the gap between a Holy God and us.

"If you believe in Him, _____ shall not perish."[43]

Perish means to die, to pass away, to suffer spiritual death.[44] We know physical death will one day happen for all of us here on earth, but the meaning in this verse is to die and be separated from God for eternity. It does not "signify cessation of existence or of consciousness."[45]

"If you believe in Him, you shall not perish,
"but _____ would have eternal life."[46]

Although this is hard to wrap our minds around, eternity is literally forever and ever and ever. We all will live for eternity. Our option is either in a literal heaven (forever in God's presence and everything good) or in a literal hell (forever separated from God with everything bad).

"God did not send his Son into the world to condemn [us]."[47] It was not about trying to point out all our sin and place shame on us. "But God demonstrates His own love for us in this: While we were still sinners, Christ died for us."[48] It was a gift He gave when we did not even deserve it. Just like the thief on the cross, our sin's consequence should be death.

_____

For God so loved

_____

that He gave
His one and only Son, [Jesus]
that if

_____

believes in Him

_____

shall not perish, but

_____

would have eternal life.

_____

What is Jesus' love like? "This is how we know what love is: Jesus Christ laid down His life for us."[49] Who would do that? "This is love: not that we loved God, but that He loved us and sent His Son as an atoning sacrifice for our sins."[50] How could Jesus' passion be so strong toward us that He would choose to die in our place, taking on our sin and giving us the gift of eternal life?

Jesus' love is relational and resolute! In a world where we have deep desires to belong, to know and be known, where people's pleasure is shifting like sand on the beach, Jesus' love is consistently solid. As I said earlier in the book, Jesus' love does not hurt. He welcomes us with open arms, without condemnation, and with great compassion. He understands us and all our deepest emotions. He knows what it is like to be hurt, to be betrayed, and to be scorned. He has experienced our pain in order to bring us comfort. He has experienced death and rose again, conquering it forever in order to bring us life.

~ ~ ~ ~ ~

"Loves Wins"

So what do we do? How do we respond to His passion for us? Some have been hurt so badly, it seems unfathomable to be accepted and loved right where you are. He knows! Some have been lied to and taken advantage of, and trust is very difficult. He saw all that—He understands! Some have had love fail them—tried that, been there, done that—no more. He heard your cries, and He cried with you!

"There is no fear in love. But perfect love drives out fear."[51] Jesus' delight in us is perfect, and no matter how many times we have been hurt in the past by others, we can trust Him. In a world where love is thrown around loosely and does not seem like something we can put our hope in, Jesus' adoration is reliable. The Bible says, "Many are the woes of the wicked, but the Lord's unfailing love surrounds the [person] who trusts in Him."[52]

> He heard your cries, and He cried with you!

"The Lord is compassionate and gracious, slow to anger, abounding in love."[53] When you are cherished like that, unconditionally, you want to love back! How do we show God our affection? "This is love for God: to obey his commands. And His commands are not burdensome."[54] "And this is love: that we walk in obedience to His commands."[55] Obedience comes in baby steps. As you saw in my story, obedience does hurt sometimes. Making those hard decisions to follow after Christ is hard. It can feel like a burden at times, but with Jesus' strength to help us, we can march on. He meets us where we are and begins to show us truth from His Word, and we take steps to obey. He knows what we can handle. He knows our heart. His love is safe and trustworthy.

So what is the bottom line? Love winning is about God's great love

> ...this is love: that we walk in obedience to His commands.

for us—not giving up on us, finding a way to reunite us in fellowship with Himself. He designed love and perfectly displayed it to us. He won the battle that Satan continues to fight. Love wins over our sin. Love wins over our eternal destiny. God's steadfast love wins—when other love fails us.

> **His love is safe and trustworthy.**

~ ~ ~ ~ ~

Truth and the Twist

Truth

God's unfailing love wins the ultimate war on sin and death.

Twist on Truth

"Love wins" when marriage is redefined; therefore,

a. I can live in the truth of that revised definition because

b. many agree on the new truth statement.

~ ~ ~ ~ ~

Untwisting Twisted Truth

The truth of "Love wins" is about perspective and where we choose to set our sights. With the new definition, truth was refocused and veiled with a screen of a limited love instead of God's unending love. Love is of God, and looking at it through His eyes, we see that love wins because He is able to reunite

His creation, whom He adores, with Himself. The greatest act of love is not us loving or marrying another human being but Jesus giving of His life so we could again come into the presence of God and spend eternity with Him in heaven.

Our victory is not in redefining love and marriage. Our true victory is this: in our sinful position, we can look to the cross, tell Jesus we believe and we are sorry for what we have done, and ask Him to take us to heaven with Him someday!

CHAPTER 18

Our Choices,
"My Life, My Rules."

This was not their first encounter. Although the rich young ruler had not spoken directly with Jesus in the past, he had lingered close enough plenty of times to overhear His teachings. The young ruler did not want to be seen mingling with the peasants and outcasts that normally held Jesus' attention. The position of authority the young ruler carried gave him opportunities to interact with the wealthy and the well-known among the land. Often listening to the Pharisees, the Jewish leaders of the day, he found their hypocritical teachings to be weak and somewhat amusing. They always found a way out of the moral fence they erected for everyone else. But something was different about this Teacher from Nazareth. The ruler was drawn to Him. Each time Jesus spoke, there was a piece of puzzling words that left the young man curious and wanting more.

As a boy, the ruler's early years had been filled with plenty of training and guidance in how to make wise decisions.

These habits became evident in his personal life as well. Each resolution was made deliberately, without haste, and carefully thought through at each step. As Jesus spoke, the ruler tried to piece the messages together. Weighing each of the teachings carefully, he considered if they were true and worthy of believing. As he continued to watch and listen from a distance, the questions plaguing his mind demanded answers. If he chose to ask, there would have to be a perfect time to get close enough to inquire.

Finally, the decision was made. He had heard enough and wanted what Jesus was talking about. Waiting for a break in the crowd, he moved closer and began to investigate. "Jesus, how do I get what You're talking about—this 'heaven'? What good thing must I do to go there?"

The Teacher turned to the rich young ruler, looked him straight in the eyes, yet saw deeper into the young man's heart. Jesus knew far more about this man than the ruler ever realized. The position that was held, the amount and love of his wealth, the prized possessions, the love of self, the prideful heart that held all these things so dear.

"Why do you ask about what is good? There is only One who is good. If you want to enter into heaven with God, you must obey the commandments."

Having been taught those as a child, he thought this might be easier than originally expected. Pressing further, he appealed, "Exactly which ones?"

Jesus began on the surface level, drawing the man closer and knowing full well the ruler already lived within the boundaries of these things. "Do not murder, do not commit adultery, do not steal, do not lie, honor your parents, and love your neighbor as yourself."

With confidence building, the man went through the list as Jesus spoke, mentally marking off each mandate. "Check. Check. Check..." For every command Jesus listed, he was one step closer to achieving the goal. Since he was accustomed to receiving exactly what he wanted, this thrilled him to know his behavior was more than satisfactory. But something was not quite right.

"I have been devoted to living out these requirements all of my life. In fact, I have been loyal to those since I was a child. But something seems to be missing. What do I lack?"

Jesus zeroed in on what was most important—the rich young ruler's heart. "Go, sell all your possessions, and give to the poor...then come, follow Me!" Although Jesus loved him and desired for him to obey, He did not force obedience. The choice would still be the man's—to follow Jesus or choose his own way.

The ruler's face immediately turned pale. Feeling lightheaded, he mentally went through an extensive inventory of belongings. "What was Jesus saying?" he questioned. "Was He serious? There is no way I could do that!"

This decision was deeper and harder than he had imagined. What first seemed like a wise decision to add heaven to his portfolio of possessions now boiled down to a choice. One of two options. Would he surrender, follow Jesus, and walk away from what was most important in his life? Or would he forfeit what he finally determined he wanted, heaven and eternal life, and choose to live by his own rules, hoping for the best, in order to keep his pride and earthly estate?

"I can't believe You are asking that of me. I just can't do it!" And with that, the ruler, with all his wealth, turned and walked away. The choice was his to make, but it cost more than he was willing to give.

Jesus turned to His disciples and took advantage of the teachable moment. "Hold the things you value lightly and be willing to let it all go in order to follow Me. I am interested in your heart and willingness to surrender your will in order to obey. People who do not have that attitude will have great difficulty entering heaven."

The disciples asked, "Then if it is so hard, how can anyone ever enter in?"

Jesus answers, "With people trying on their own, making up their own rules as they go along, this is impossible. But, with God, all things are possible! Obedience—dealing with your own private idols—cannot be accomplished on your own. God is able to do the impossible as you surrender, offering your all to Him. But it is up to you—your choice."

Adapted from Matthew 19:16–30

~ ~ ~ ~ ~

The Biblical Truth

While the slogan "My life, my rules" is not unique to the LGBTQ, they share the underlining thought process of doing things "my way" along with many of us. As we have seen earlier, this is nothing new to mankind but has been our desire and a tactic of Satan from the beginning of time. It feels good to be in charge. We want to have a bit of power, especially when circumstances in our lives are falling apart and seem out of our control.

If we have been a victim of abuse or had any kind of situation where someone took advantage of us, it seems unimaginable that we would be asked or even willing to give up control to a God who could have stepped in and changed our circumstances.

I cannot explain why God allowed me to go through being molested as a young teen, then allowing my friend's death and Mom's cancer, which led me into being molested again. But I have come to believe that even in the midst of my pain and difficulty, I was never alone. God did not want those things to happen to me, yet He did not create robots that He would manipulate. The people who hurt me were also born in sin and had free will. They chose poorly, and as a result, I was hurt.

...choosing to follow Christ brought me freedom and peace that I could never have experienced while living in bondage to sin.

But God is still God, and He can take those horrible life situations and use them to help bring comfort to others and introduce them to Jesus. Through it all, I have seen His hand at work guiding me to places and people where I could see what His love really looked like. He protected me from killing myself. He led me to Christ-followers who would love me and help me through the difficulty of walking away from homosexuality. He provided for my physical needs and made a way for me to complete my education. Yes, there was pain along the way. Yes, obedience cost me a great deal. But choosing to follow Christ brought me freedom and peace that I could never have experienced while living in bondage to sin. As I fell in love with Jesus, my desire to follow Him grew. Walking in obedience and daily surrendering to His will was worth the struggles along the way.

~ ~ ~ ~ ~

God, as Creator of the universe and everything that exists, has the right to set up the rules for how things will be. He is the Giver of life and has guidelines for us, His creation. He has the plan and openly shares it with us through His Word. As we saw earlier, "the wages of sin is death, but the gift of God is eternal life in Christ Jesus our Lord."[56] Jesus gave His life, and the free gift is available and waiting for our decision. Will we repent of our sin, choose to accept His gift, and receive abundant life now and a future in heaven? Or will we reject His offer and choose, instead, to spend eternity in hell? It is a free gift in that there is nothing we can do to earn it. But it will cost us as we surrender our lives and our wills in order to take the next step toward obedience to His ways. "This is love for God: to obey His commands."[57]

So what does that even look like? Do we have to fix everything in our lives and clean up to come to Jesus? Not at all! Realizing we are a sinner and in need of God's grace, we repent, agreeing with what He calls sin, and we come to Him—just as we are. He is just waiting to be invited into your life, and when He is, He will take care of the cleaning part. The Bible says if we confess our sin, He forgives us and cleanses us from all unrighteousness.[58] He washes us, making us whiter than snow.[59] He wants to be a part of your everyday life, but He will not push His way in. You have a choice. Jesus says, "Here I am! I stand at the door [of your heart] and knock. If anyone hears My voice and opens the door, I will come in and eat with him, and he with Me."[60]

How do you know He is there? How do you hear His knocking and His voice? Sometimes, it is simply that racing heartbeat that indicates to you a sense of knowing you need to do something right away. Sometimes it is a gentle tugging deep inside your soul, where your gut is telling you that you need to follow through with this. Ask Him to make His voice known to you. If you are a little scared and maybe a bit unsure of what it all means, it is all right to tell Him. You are precious to Him, and He pursues those created in His image with an everlasting love. Remember He is crazy about you!

The Bible says, "If we confess our sins, He is faithful and just and will forgive us our sins and purify us from all unrighteousness."[61] But "if we claim we have not sinned, we make Him out to be a liar and His word has no place in our lives."[62] "God is light; in Him there is no darkness at all. If we claim to have fellowship with Him yet walk in the darkness, we lie and do not live by the truth."[63] When we confess our sin, acknowledging our need for Jesus, we surrender ourselves to Him and ask Him to be in control of and guide our lives. We may not understand fully, but He is patient with us and will love us right where we are as we learn to walk in obedience to Him.

His invitation to us is: "Come and follow." Jesus never forces obedience—it is always our choice. Our love for Him will be

> He is patient with us and will love us right where we are as we learn to walk in obedience to Him.

revealed through our obedience and choosing to follow close after Him. When we answer, "Yes, Lord," we are trusting Him for each step we take. We do not have to understand it all. We do not have to figure it all out. He just calls us to trust and obey.

Many times in life we have our list of accomplishments. The resume looks good, our finances give us some security, and our homes and vacations display abundance, but we still come up short. True, inner peace alludes us, and we ask ourselves, What am I missing? So we keep searching, keep climbing the corporate ladder, and keep working harder, but there is still an emptiness that we just cannot fill. However, when we take our focus off of "me," "all I have," and "all I have done," we will begin to see the truth because it is then that we are willing to ask the harder question, "God, what do I lack?"

~ ~ ~ ~ ~

Truth and the Twist

Truth

God designed our lives, made us, and has the master plan as Creator.

Twist on Truth

I am the boss of my life and will determine my own destiny; therefore,

a. I can do what I want when I want, where I want, and how I want, and

b. I am in control of what happens in my life, both now and for eternity.

~ ~ ~ ~ ~

Untwisting Twisted Truth

Just like the rich young ruler, we want to do life our own way, with our own rules, yet we are not the Creator but His created beings. God is the master Creator. He made us and waits for us to choose to love Him in return. The beginning of untwisting what has been so confusingly twisted is to acknowledge God as the One who made us and who has the master plan for all of mankind.

Obedience requires action. Acting obediently requires repentance and sacrifice. Sacrifice of myself and my will. We often want to do it our own way, or we continue seeking to find a way around the truth. Sometimes it seems too painful or scary to surrender. It will not come easy, but it is possible. Remember...all things are possible—with God![64]

There are some questions we all have to ask ourselves...

• *Will I choose to love God by obeying Him or turn my back on Him and walk away?*

> Acting obediently requires repentance and sacrifice. Sacrifice of myself and my will.

- *Will I choose to repent of my sin to follow His path for my life or chart my own course?*
- *Will I choose to surrender my life to His master plan or live (and die) with the consequences?*

My choices determine how I will live my life and where I will spend eternity. God did not make me a robot that has to love Him. I have a choice.

~ ~ ~ ~ ~

When that time comes and you sense God knocking on the door of your heart, here is a prayer you can pray to ask Him in. It does not have to be these exact words. You just have to be sincere and mean it.

~ ~ ~ ~ ~

Dear Jesus, I know I am a sinner and have broken Your rules. I believe You died on the cross to pay the penalty for my sin and to make a way for me to go to heaven someday. Please fortive me and come into my heart. I surrender my life to You. I do not understand it all, but I ask you go give me strength and teach me how to obey You. Thank You for the gift of eternal life. In Jesus' name, amen.

———————

Dear Jesus,
I know I am a sinner and
have broken Your rules.
I believe You died
on the cross to
pay the penalty for my sin and
to make a way for me
to go to heaven someday.
Please forgive me and
come into my heart.
I surrender my life to You.
I do not understand it all,
but I ask You to
give me strength and
teach me how to obey You.
Thank You for the gift
of eternal life.
In Jesus' name, amen.

———————

~ ~ ~ ~ ~

When you ask Jesus to come into your heart and life, He comes in to stay. He promises, "Never will I leave you; never will I forsake you."[65] There is nothing you have done that is too bad for Him to forgive. Once He comes in, there is nothing you can do to make Him leave. If you prayed that prayer, you are now a child of God, and no one can ever take that away from you. Oh, and just so you know—if you prayed that prayer, there is a party going on in heaven! "There is rejoicing in the presence of the angels of God over one sinner who repents."[66] Jesus is crazy about you!

CHAPTER 19

Our Identity, "We're Here, We're Queer."

The invitations were out. Angels extraordinaire Gabriel and Michael were given permission to plan a party—a celebration of transformation. The instructions were for everyone to come in their BC attire with costumes and masks of what their lives looked like "before Christ." As they gathered together, each would be given a chance to share how their life had been touched by Jesus' love and changed forever. They called it *A Night to Remember!*

Gabriel and Michael could hardly contain their excitement. Having always known Jesus, they had never experienced Him bringing change to their existence like those who would be attending the party. Although they were privileged to have been involved in a few of the life transformations, many were handled with the other angels' assistance. These stories had circulated around heaven when the people walked from bondage to freedom, and tonight, the angels gathered to rejoice again— just as they had when these people first put their trust in Jesus.

Excitement grew as everyone arrived and took their seats in the exquisitely decorated banquet room. As people came to share their stories, they approached from the left, where a red carpet led the way to center stage. This carpet symbolized Jesus' blood that was shed on the cross, laid out before them as a precious reminder of His love. The path was for all who had chosen to believe and put their trust in Jesus, not just for the elite, because there are no elite in heaven. All had sinned, and all came to the cross on level ground—not one better than the other.

One by one, they came, masquerading as their former selves. Stepping up to the microphone, each shared their story of a broken life that had been mended by the Great Healer and Lover of their soul. Upon the completion of their story, Jesus joined them. They knelt before Him, and He removed their foreign mask to reveal their true identity—for it was by this identity, as seen through Jesus' eyes, that they were known! He raised them up, rejoicing with them because they no longer carried their sins and labels of the past but were pure and righteous and free. The applause exploded every time—each experience just as powerful as the last as they rejoiced in what Jesus had done.

Exiting stage right, surrounded by white, glistening clouds of angels, everyone was in awe of the radical change. Nothing was more telling than their eyes and the countenance of their faces. The demeanor in which they carried themselves made each of them look like a different person. In fact, they were completely made new because the old self, with all the baggage, was washed away, and a brand-new life had come. They were set free!

Some of those compelling stories include the following...

Peter had arrived with a fishing net slung over his shoulder and a sword in his hand. His weathered mask had a large mouth and fearful eyes. His shoulders drooped in shame, and he shook his head, wondering if all he had believed was for nothing. Jesus had set him free from fear and shame, restoring his confidence as Peter confirmed his love for Jesus three times.

A woman came carrying a bucket. There was loneliness and despair in her eyes, which were hidden most of the time by the long scarf wrapped strategically to hide her identity from the judging gazes of others. She held disgrace and guilt close in her clenched fists. Her freedom had come as Jesus exposed the truths of her life, yet loved and accepted her, giving her new life as she left to tell everyone about Him.

No one was ready for what came next. Screaming and yelling and chains dragging on the ground. This guy was crazy! He ran in circles as he made his way on stage. His matted hair with painted bruises and cuts on his body helped everyone recognize who this was. Thankfully, the man from the graveyard had wrapped a towel around himself, hiding his shorts. His acting ability was incredible as many marveled at his deranged behavior. When Jesus had told the demon to leave him, he had been set free and was given a renewed mind to go along with his physical makeover.

Another woman cried out, "Unclean," as she entered. Her body was weak from the disease that lasted so many years. She, too, covered her face with her outer garment, trying to hide. Unwanted in public, her worthlessness, emptiness, and pain came through loud and clear as she spoke. Her mask displayed evidence of oppression, mournful eyes, and a heaping measure of discouragement. Her hope of healing had caused her to risk more condemnation as she pushed through the crowd to touch the hem of Jesus' garment. Freed through her faith in the power of touching Jesus—He called her "daughter."

The last man seemed about as crazy as the one from the graveyard. He came with official orders and shouted at the top of his lungs. Carrying some chains, he approached various people before going on stage, asking if they were followers of Jesus. Saul was looking for believers to capture and throw into jail. His mask was full of pride and anger all mixed together. Blinded by the truth of his sin on the road to Damascus, Saul had been set free, his name changed to Paul, and his passion in life was drastically altered.

What an amazing time. Each one's *true identity* broadcast for eternity. This! This is who they actually are! It was absolutely breathtaking. Definitely *a night to remember!*

Adapted from Luke 15:10

~ ~ ~ ~ ~

The Biblical Truth

Long before you drew a breath, God peered through the timeline of birth announcements and called you by name. He knew your eye color, your hair color, your quirks, and your talents. You were His idea from the beginning. He crafted you together in the womb, known only to Him, even before your mother realized you existed. Who you would be, what you would do—all was familiar to God prior to your birth. Your character and personality were celebrated by the God of the universe. You are distinctive and distinguished from others by your identity, but sometimes the perception of identity can become distorted. When we believe what others say about us and what we think of ourselves, our hearts and minds are bound up as Satan twists the truth.

We may not recognize our bondage nor realize our need for freedom from false ideologies. We have been told things that have shifted and redefined the original true identity God imprinted on our souls. Satan has thrown confusion and deceit into the mix of "who am I?" But truth can be found in the person of Jesus Christ. As we examine the Bible, Jesus speaks of Himself as the way, the truth, and the life.[67] Truth will set us free![68]

Looking at the biblical characters in the drama from Jesus' point of view, we see quite a different picture of their identity. In Peter, Jesus did not see the coward who shrank back when it was time to stand up for Him. He did not see the man who spoke before thinking, saying exactly what was on his mind. He saw Peter as a rock, a strong preacher who would tell others about the truth he had come to know and believe.[69]

As the woman who had been married several times and was now living with yet another man came near Jesus at the well, He saw her wounded, broken heart. He knew the many times she had cried herself to sleep as each man left her, making her feel worthless, unwanted, and unloved. Jesus knew exactly what she needed—not another man, not another scornful look, but truth blanketed in love. He knew her lifestyle and the labels she wore. He told her that her character was not found in her

> Her identity would never be found in her sexuality! Her distinctiveness would be found in Christ alone.

identification by those labels. Her identity would never be found in her sexuality! Her distinctiveness would be found in Christ alone. He called her to genuine worship as she pursued truth. Who she was and the way she lived were what mattered most.[70]

Each one came with broken pieces of who they thought they were—lies they believed—trying to define their existence by what they did or what people said about them. We will always be on an endless search for our identity until we can accept who we are in Christ and choose to see ourselves through His eyes. Loved. Forgiven. Accepted. Chosen.

It is not a matter of being gay, straight, adulterer, or trans; those identify your behavior, but not who you are—all of that is secondary. What matters foremost, as you hold up the mirror to gaze into your soul, is that you are loved deeply by the God who made you. You must choose to listen to who *He* says you are. As we come to know who we are in Christ first, the rest of the things begin to fall into place. You are not who you have been told you are by family, friends, or those who hurt you. Rather, Jesus calls you "daughter" or "son."[71]

All too often, we not only carry those identifying adjectives placed on us by others, but we allow them to seep into the very essence of our being. Shame, unclean, guilty, disappointment, gay, stupid, queer, worthless, loser...need I go on? Why is it so much easier to replay the negative voices and soundtracks in our mind than the positive ones? Why are these the labels that scream the loudest to us through our own self-talk? Will we choose to continue to listen to them and give them space to rent on the property of our minds?[72]

No more! We have listened to the lies long enough. It is time to tune our ears to God's gentle whisper. What does our Creator, the One who designed and made us, have to say about who we are? Who does Jesus see as He looks at you?

~ ~ ~ ~ ~

Who Am I?

> We will always be on an endless search for our identity until we can accept who we are in Christ and choose to see ourselves through His eyes. Loved. Forgiven. Accepted. Chosen.

While struggling with some labels of my own, God led me to Psalm 139 and revealed some truths about my identity. Here are excerpts of the chapter with my prayers as I worked through the truth of who Jesus says I am. I invite you to join me and view yourself through the lens of God's Word.

Psalm 139:1–5 (NIV):

O Lord, You have searched me and You know me.

You know when I sit and when I rise;

You perceive my thoughts from afar.

You discern my going out and my lying down;

You are familiar with all my ways.

Before a word is on my tongue

You know it completely, O Lord.

You hem me in—behind and before;

You have laid Your hand upon me.

"I am *known!* At the very deepest part of my being, God, You know me! Lord, that is exactly what I have always longed for. You know my thoughts. You understand why and where those thoughts come from. You hear my self-talk. You see how I perceive myself. Before I speak a word, You are aware of what I am going to say—about others or about myself. You appreciate what makes my cadence unique. You grasp what triggers my fears. You discern the direction my thoughts take me and the pit of lies I camp in at times. You get me! You know all about me, and yet You won't leave me! With full knowledge of all those thoughts, perceptions, beliefs, and ideologies, You say, 'I know, My child. I understand.' You hem me in—not to confine but to love and protect. You give me a giant 'God hug'!"

> My identity—
> designed from
> the inside out!

Psalm 139:13–16 (NIV):

For you created my inmost being;
You knit me together in my mother's womb.
I praise You because
I am fearfully and wonderfully made;
Your works are wonderful, I know that full well.
My frame was not hidden from You
when I was made in the secret place.
When I was woven together in the depths of the earth,
Your eyes saw my unformed body.

"Lord, I was Your idea from the beginning. You thought me up. You created me. Not only were You the Designer, but You were also the Manufacturer. You were intentional as You knit me together. You put all my pieces and parts together. Nothing was left out, nothing forgotten, no leftover scraps—all perfectly planned. Then, You packaged me in the exact body You chose for my earthly existence. No mistakes, no oops, no plan B. Pure excellence in Your eyes! Your works are wonderful. And I am one of Your works. Give me Your eyes to see Your wonderful work when I look in the mirror. Let me never forget my beginning—a twinkle in Your eye.

"God, I was not hidden from You. You were with me there in secret, breathing Your design into every little detail—starting from the inside and working Your way out. From conception, my DNA was set, and my gender and features already determined. You designed my inner parts first—who I am, my identity—before You ever put the final layer of skin on. My *identity*—designed from the inside out!"

Psalm 139:19–22 (NIV):

If only You would slay the wicked, O God!
Away from me, you bloodthirsty men!
They speak of You with evil intent;
Your adversaries misuse Your name.
Do I not hate those who hate You, O Lord,
and abhor those who rise up against You?
I have nothing but hatred for them;
I count them my enemies.

"God, life is hard! As I look at Your Word as a whole, I know You want us to love others and not hate them. But in the midst of this chapter, it appears as though You are showing me a picture of how You designed me, but evil people came along, slapping labels on me that have become a part of who I am and how I see myself. I have carried those adjectives with me for many days. Lord, I know it is okay to not like what people do when they hurt me! Evil people, masquerading as friends and lovers, have attacked me, Your beautiful creation, through their words and deeds. They spoke evil against who You made and intended me to be. I hate that and what it has done to me! I hate the lies that their actions have caused me to believe about myself!"

Psalm 139:23–24 (NIV):

Search me, O God, and know my heart;
Test me and know my anxious thoughts.
See if there is any offensive way in me,
And lead me in the way everlasting.

God expose in me and remove:
Any offensive thought…
Any offensive idea…
Any offensive belief…
Any offensive talk…
…That goes against who You designed and made me to be!

"Lord, search the depths of my soul. Know what is in my heart. Examine my anxious thoughts—what are they specifically, and where do they come from? What are the thoughts and words inside me that offend You? Am I believing lies from man? Am I believing lies I have repeated to myself? Am I believing lies from Satan, the true enemy, that are offensive to You?

"God, I am so sorry. Please forgive me for believing the lies. It makes sense that You would take offense at someone speaking badly of me or doing evil against me, Your wonderful work. I am Your child, and it hurts You when I am wounded.

"Lord, send Your 'Search and Rescue Angels' to shine a light where I hide things from You. Shine where I might defend the ugly words about myself because, after all, I have believed them for a long time. Shine where I might blow off someone's actions that hurt deeply and made me see myself through their false perception. Rescue my wounded heart, bringing me to repentance and forgiveness, and may You breathe life into me again! Make the offenses known. Expose the things that go against You and Your design for me. Then, lead me in the way of *truth!*"

God, expose in me and remove:

Any offensive thought...

Any offensive idea...

Any offensive belief...

Any offensive talk...

...That goes against who
You designed and made me to be!

~ ~ ~ ~ ~

Truth and the Twist

Truth

1. God made me, and He doesn't make mistakes.
2. The foundation of my identity is who Jesus says I am.

Twist on Truth—Part One

1. God made a mistake when He made me; therefore,
2. my changing identity is based on whoever I think I am today.

Twist on Truth—Part Two

1. I am what I have done and what others have done to me;
2. I am my past mistakes;
3. I am what I have (my talent, my looks, my possessions);
4. I am who others say I am; therefore,
    a. the lies I believe because of the pain in my life are to blame for my behavior, and
    b. I can never change my view of myself or my behavior, so get used to it.

~ ~ ~ ~ ~

Untwisting Twisted Truth

In a current dictionary, "the use of queer avoids any specific label." Yet, it is defined as "strange or odd from a conventional viewpoint; of a questionable nature or character; suspicious;

———————

Rescue my wounded heart,
bringing me to
repentance and
forgiveness,
and may You breathe life
into me again!
Make the offenses known.
Expose the things
that go against You and
Your design for me.
Then, lead me
in the way of truth!

———————

shady; mentally unbalanced or deranged."[73] Based on that definition, God has loved, healed, and called many queer people into a relationship with Himself in the past, just as He does today. The moment of truth comes as we see ourselves as Jesus does—first as a sinner in need of His grace, then forgiven and righteous. There is no cookie-cutter mold of who we should be, look like, or act like, yet Jesus calls us to holiness as He is holy.[74] He longs to have a relationship with us regardless of where we fall on the "queer meter."

Our model, who we look to for our holiness, influence, and identity is Jesus Christ. To untwist what Satan had twisted in my life, I made a list of the labels others had put on me over the years. Not too surprisingly, I found they were adjectives I used often to define myself. Continuing to study Psalm 139, I realized my list was offensive to the God who made me. Those words were not what He saw when He looked at me. Asking God to give me eyes to see from His perspective, I began looking up each word in a thesaurus to find the opposite meaning. Before I read through the list of antonyms, I prayed for God to reveal which one best described the truth of how He saw me. Next to my original list, I wrote the antonyms in red that God pointed out to me and which resonated within my spirit. These adjectives are what Jesus sees when He looks at me! It was so encouraging to view this list and begin to read these out loud to help me redefine

> Our model, who we look to for our holiness, influence, and identity is Jesus Christ.

who I saw myself as. Giving further support to these new words, I again asked God to reveal scripture that spoke to the truth that was being revealed. Using a glossary in the back of my Bible and my Bible app, I found and wrote out the verses that spoke truth about who I am. I encourage you to give it a try. (See appendix B.[75]) Speak the truth about who you were made to be. Untwist the lies and put some new labels on your life! Read these new labels with the scriptures out loud daily until you begin to believe the truth of who you are in Christ.

As we catch those negative thoughts and replace them with how Jesus sees us, our lives will be changed more into His likeness. "I am convinced and confident of this very thing, that He who has begun a good work in you will [continue to] perfect and complete it until the day of Christ Jesus [the time of His return]."[76]

CHAPTER 20

Our Vulnerability, Just Like the LGBTQ

"Game on! If God thinks I am just going to back down and not fight for my rights, He's got another thing coming! I deserve the position of power! I deserve to be worshipped; after all, I am the most beautiful angel in heaven—at least...I was. He will be sorry He messed with me! If I cannot get at Him directly, I will go after His Son, Jesus, and those He created in His image, His 'precious human beings.' He thinks they will worship Him and want to follow Him. I've got a few plans up my sleeve that will derail that lame idea. I will not stop until I get them to turn their backs on God and follow me. He said I would lose in the end. If He is right, I am not going down without a fight—and if I am going down, I am taking as many of His creations with me as I can!"

Satan's mind was made up—to fight at any cost. When he had been thrown out of heaven, he took one-third of the angels with him. They were now under his command, and they worshipped this fallen angel. Satan enjoyed his position on the throne of their hearts, but he would not rest until he gathered as many humans as he could to add to his following. His fight against God would be the zenith of all battles lasting throughout all the ages. "Bring it on!"

His thoughts were jerked back to the present as his generals arrived. They had gathered for a meeting to discuss the progress of this week's focal points. Things were moving along quite smoothly. In fact, they were accelerating at an exceptional speed, and there was much to celebrate. But celebrations would have to wait—they knew letting up on the pressure was not an option.

"All right, let's get started. We do not have a lot of time to waste. Time equals souls—and we need more!" Although Satan was extremely patient in waiting for the right moment to bring an attack on the humans, he was impatient when it came to hearing how wonderful his plans were going.

Through the years, Satan had perfected the art of choosing his victims carefully. He was highly skilled as he identified the vulnerable ones in a crowd. All the demons had been well-trained and prided themselves in picking the easiest targets, patiently waiting for the ideal time to make their move: after a poor decision, as someone became complacent, during relationship issues...the opportunities were endless. Once in a while, the demons caused a confusing and chaotic scene where people would scatter from connectedness with each other. The weakest and most vulnerable were left straggling behind, alone. That was the simplest time to lure them into a trap.

Whether young or old, the plan was always to separate them and get them isolated from others, either physically or emotionally. At the point of unguarded behavior, they were defenseless to the enemy's attack. Each life-giving breath slowly snuffed out as they suffocated right in the midst of thinking everything was fine. The kiss of death began very innocently but always proved to be a clean-cut way to overpower the victim until they succumbed to the enemy's influence. There were all sorts of tactics: anger at God, doubt that God cared, loss of relationships, loss of innocence, hurt feelings…each time, the Prince of Darkness scored as his team of demons drew another unsuspecting victim away from falling in love with Jesus and following God.

They brainstormed about the next phase of action. Many offered good suggestions, all with profitable possibilities. But one thing bothered Satan above anything else—those followers of Jesus were learning to love the sinners more like Jesus did. That was going to be a problem because if the people saw how much Jesus loved them, they might actually believe His story of grace and want to follow Him as well. Satan and the demons went round and round, discussing ideas for the next attack until they were almost at a standstill. Then, one of them had an idea that just might do the trick.

The demon began cautiously, "What if we go ahead and let them love on the sinners but work on twisting their perception of that love? I mean, if they perceived the Christ-followers as judging and condemning them, we could cause more confusion and tremendous misunderstandings so that both sides would get angry. We could also distort the Christian's perception of their own sin, thinking they are invincible to certain sins, making them more vulnerable to our attacks. This will cause them to say things that will get twisted and come out wrong, ultimately causing any potential believer to end up hating them and the Christ they serve."

Satan had been pacing back and forth nervously, yet as the innovative idea began to take shape, he slowed to take it all in and absorb the enormity of possibilities. "Could it really be that simple? Just adjust both sides' perceptions? Brilliant!"

Adapted from 1 Peter 5:8

~ ~ ~ ~ ~

The Biblical Truth

When my boys were little, the older one would chase the younger one around the house, ready to pounce at the perfect opportunity in order to tackle him to the ground. This did not continue long before the younger one wised up to the game and came up with a plan.

They had recently watched *The Incredibles* movie where each member of the Incredible family had a different superpower they used to help people and fight off evil. To my surprise, my younger son pulled a strong tactic from the movie to use on his older brother. Right about the time the youngest was about to be taken down, he would suddenly stop running, quickly turn to his brother, hold his hand up with the palm firmly in a "stop" position, and confidently yell, "Force field!" This caused the oldest to halt mid-stride and defeatedly shake his head as he was foiled again. Yielding, he would cry out, "Oh, maaaan!" They would rest a while as the younger one nonchalantly crept a few feet away before the chase started once again.

Over and over, the game ensued with the youngest being able to stop the attack with a simple gesture and two words. I laughed at their little game, yet God reminded me of some incredible truths through their play.

~ ~ ~ ~ ~

Satan is real and we are under attack.

The first truth is that Satan is real and we are under attack. Every age group is vulnerable, but especially the hearts and minds of children through young adults. That is a battleground where Satan is not willing to give up. Whether we are a Christ-follower, not yet a believer, or an individual wanting nothing to do with God at all, Satan longs for our attention to be turned away from anything remotely connected to Jesus.

The apostle Peter tells us, "Be self-controlled and alert. Your enemy the devil prowls around like a roaring lion looking for someone to devour."[77] Satan is on the hunt! He is sniffing out our weaknesses, tracking down what trips us up the most, and seeking our allegiance in any degree he can. We are being adamantly pursued.

The warning is not just for the weak and wounded. It is also for the ones who think it could never happen to them. The complacent. The spiritual. The ones who get comfortable in their Christian walk and scoff at those who have fallen into sin's trap. It is all too easy to look at others and say, "Their sin is much worse than mine. I don't know how they could ever do that." Yet, Peter has a warning to us all: "Hey, watch out! Pay attention!"

~ ~ ~ ~ ~

The prowling techniques are intense in the lion hunt. Whether sneaking in a cat-like walk, lingering behind trees or tall grass, spying out the weak and needy, or crouching close before an actual attack, the lions are very intentional. At times, they wait near water because they know the prey will eventually come to quench their thirst. If the lions are noticed as they lie in wait, they will sit up tall and look off in the distance like their focus was really on something else all along until the prey relaxes, goes back to grazing, and ignores the impending danger.

When the initial lion attacks, it goes for the throat, crushing the windpipe and squeezing off the airflow, thereby suffocating the prey. Latching onto the throat, with front legs wrapped around the animal's neck, it looks like a giant hug, but the lion hangs on with this "kiss of death" until life is taken. If it cannot get to the throat, other lions join in quickly to take the prey down as they cover the snout, stopping any possibility of taking the next breath.[78]

The comparison of Satan prowling after us like a lion is enough to make anyone leery of ever stepping out of their home. So should we live in fear and search for a demon behind every door? Not at all. But we need to be watchful, aware of our own weaknesses, and alert when something does not seem quite right or is not lining up with God's Word. The Bible warns, "See to it that no one takes you captive through hollow and deceptive philosophy, which depends on human tradition and the basic principles of this world rather than on Christ."[79] Acknowledging our dependence on God for help, staying connected in a church community with other Christ-followers, and finding a couple of friends with whom we can be vulnerable and who will hold us accountable will do a great deal to help us walk with an awareness of the enemy's schemes.

~ ~ ~ ~ ~

The other incredible truth I realized as I watched my boys play was how we need to more effectively use our force field of God's protection through prayer. For the boys, as long as the younger one was using his force field to protect himself, he could not be touched and felt confident stopping his older brother. Likewise, as the older one heard there was a force field in place, his little brother was off limits. The major contrast between their play and our lives is that our battle and need for a force field to ward off the enemy's attacks is indeed very real.

Praying for God's protection does not mean that life will be without problems. We live in a sinful world and walk through the consequences of people's choices. But as we do, His presence is with us to strengthen us and help us through.

God is our refuge and defense. Paul tells us to

> put on the full armor of God [for His precepts are like the splendid armor of a heavily-armed soldier], so that you may be able to [successfully] stand up against all the schemes and the strategies and the deceits of the devil. For our struggle is not against flesh and blood [contending only with physical opponents], but against the rulers, against the powers, against the world forces

of this [present] darkness, against the spiritual forces of wickedness in the heavenly (supernatural) places. Therefore, put on the complete armor of God, so that you will be able to [successfully] resist and stand your ground in the evil day [of danger], and having done everything [that the crisis demands], to stand firm [in your place, fully prepared, immovable, victorious].[80]

The power of God's armor protecting us and praying a shield of faith over us (like my son's force field) makes us bold. We are called to "be strong in the Lord [draw your strength from Him and be empowered through your union with Him] and in the power of His [boundless] might."[81]

The armor God supplies and makes available to us does not provide anything to protect our backs. We are not to cower in fear, running away from the battle, but we resist and firmly stand our ground. As we face the enemy who is trying to ensnare us, we hold up the shield of faith and pray as God's "force field" surrounds us. We are standing up to the enemy, and he is defeated because of God's power. But Satan does not give up easily and will continue to attack, trying to gain victory over us. We have a need to daily put on our armor to fight him, covering each day in prayer.

~ ~ ~ ~ ~

Truth and the Twist

Truth

We all are vulnerable to Satan's snares and need to be alert to his schemes.

Twist on Truth

We all are vulnerable, and my sin of pride, for example, could easily be ignored; therefore,

    a. the visible sins of the LGBTQ and others may look worse than my sin, which I keep hidden or do not recognize exists, and

    b. the condemnation I might feel toward them is justified because their sin is obviously worse than mine.

~ ~ ~ ~ ~

<u>Untwisting Twisted Truth</u>

I will never forget the day I was walking into a restaurant with my then-teenage sons as we discussed a recent news story of a well-known athlete who was now transgender. I told my boys we were just like him. Immediately, one of my boys spun around so fast I thought he would fall over. He said, "I am *not* like that person!" This made for a very interesting conversation over dinner.

> ...we all have the potential to be snared by thoughts that are twisted from the truth, especially during vulnerable points of our lives.

My point was—we all have the potential to be snared by thoughts that are twisted from the truth, especially during vulnerable points of our lives. But it is easy to look at someone doing something we may not necessarily agree with and think, *I would never...* In reality, we do not know what we would do until we are in their situation. I surely had never expected to be walking down the pathway of homosexuality, but in a time of vulnerability, my guard was down, and I ignored the truth.

John Bradford, an English evangelical preacher and martyr, is credited with what I have heard many times throughout the years, "There but for the grace of God, go I!"[82] The enemy would like to trip all of us up in one way or another. We all have areas of weakness; some are just more visible than others. May we realize our own vulnerability, and may God give us increased compassion to love those who have been lured into sin of one kind or another.

> We all have areas of weakness; some are just more visible than others.

As we seek the Lord with a surrendered heart, we can best prepare for the enemy's attack by daily putting on the complete armor of God. What does it look like to put on God's armor? Here is an example of my armored prayer you could use, which is adapted from Ephesians 6:10–20 and goes something like this:

"Precious Jesus,

"Thank You for being my refuge and strength. You are a very present help in times of trouble. Thank You for being my defender and providing me with armor that can protect me against the enemy's schemes. My battle is not against flesh and blood, but it is against the powers and rulers of darkness and against the spiritual forces of wickedness. *Today, I choose to put on Your armor and claim Your victory.*

"First, I put on the **BELT OF TRUTH** because everything else hinges on this piece. Thank You for the visual You gave me of this many years ago as I defended my opponent playing basketball. My eyes were always fixed on her midsection because, although she could throw a fake with other parts of her body, where her core went was always where the rest of her body was going.

"Lord, in the same way, where truth goes, that is where I will follow. Help me walk in the truth of Your Word today. Help me listen to truth, both from others as well as in my self-talk. Help my thoughts to be true; help me to believe truth and speak truth. The enemy would want to twist the truth and throw lies in the midst of my thoughts. Help me sift those thoughts through the truth of Your Word. *Protect my direction.*

"Next, I put on the **BREASTPLATE OF RIGHTEOUSNESS** and integrity. Guide my heart to choose to act on what is right in Your eyes. Attacks will come against my heart, my beliefs, my emotions, and my self-esteem. I lay them all at Your feet and am reminded that I am made righteous because of Your love and sacrifice on the cross. My righteousness is none of my doing, but it is complete in You. May I walk in integrity whether anyone watches or not. Let it be a part of who I am because of who You have made me to be. *Protect my emotions, self-worth, and heart—not falling prey to the enemy's lies.*

"**COVER MY FEET**, Lord, with an unswerving loyalty that is swift and steady, balanced and unwavering. Make my feet resolute, firmly determined to walk in Your ways. Help me live decidedly, setting my path in the way of obedience. Unshakable. Uncompromising. Unflinching. Steadfast in purpose to be prepared to share the Gospel of peace. Cover my feet with protection for where I will walk with You today. Let my feet not get snared in any traps that would try to slow me down or detour my way. Make my feet sure-footed, stable, and prompt in my obedience and readiness to share the Gospel. *Protect my passion for telling others of Your love and grace.*

"I lift up my **SHIELD OF FAITH**, my covering, with which to quench the flaming missiles of the wicked one. I cannot stop the enemy from attacking me, but I can stand protected. Give me the strength I need to hold it up. Where I struggle to believe, increase my faith. Surround me with people who will join together with me and to whom I can help support. Help me when I am weak and tempted to lower my shield of faith when I am tempted to give in to my doubts, my worries, my concerns. I submit those all to You and ask You to help me trust in Your deliverance. *Protect me from unguarded attacks.*

"I put on the **HELMET OF SALVATION** and ask that You protect my mind. Jesus, the enemy would like nothing more than for me to doubt You and wonder if what You say is true. Thank You for my salvation and for having made a way for me to live forever secure in Your presence. God, You give me the mind of Christ, and I ask for clarity in my thinking and to be focused on You. *Protect me from false thoughts, opinions, and attacks on my mind.*

"I hold up the **SWORD OF THE SPIRIT**, which is the Word of God. I am ready for battle, cutting through lies and anything attempting to come between You and me. Bring to my memory those verses I have hidden in my heart and the truths that have been spoken over me. *Let me cling to Your truth and trust in You alone.*

"I cover all of this with **PRAYER** and ask that You will dwell with me—Your presence creating a hunger that leads me to follow Your Spirit. Thank You for Your protection. Lead me on today, Lord. In the powerful name of Jesus, amen."[83]

~ ~ ~ ~ ~

"Submit yourselves, then, to God.
Resist the devil, and he will flee from you."[84]

CHAPTER 21

Our Calling, Just Like Jesus

Oh, what she would give to be invisible at this moment! Choices—some she made; some made by others. If she could only turn back the hands of time and rewrite this scene, rewrite last night, this year, the last five years. Maybe things would be different. Maybe she would not be standing here, disgraced for adultery and about to be stoned. But here she was—thrown into the middle of the courtyard in front of the growing crowd, many of whom she had known all her life. And there was Jesus. She had not taken time to listen to Him before, but she knew others who had. In fact, her mother had asked on several occasions for her to join the family as they went to the countryside to hear Jesus teach. She did not have time for that then. Today, however, she wondered what He had to say. Did He care as much as people said He did?

A tear ran down her cheek as the men told Jesus what she had done. She could not look at Him. Her eyes downcast, her face flushed. She repeated the words over and over in her head, "Breathe. Hold on a little longer. Just breathe."

No one really cared about her needs right now. Many gathered around out of curiosity. They were interested in what Jesus' response would be to the teachers of the law and Pharisees who brought her as a pawn in hopes that Jesus would speak falsely against the law. The crowd wanted to witness it for themselves. Although stoning was the normal punishment for this situation, everyone wondered how Jesus would address it today.

As the religious leaders yelled and voiced their opinions, no one listened to her or even considered the fact that she just wanted to be held and loved.

As they pushed Jesus for an answer, hoping to trip Him up, no one cared about the fact that she had been hungry and would always be given something to eat after she had satisfied "his" needs.

As they picked up their stones, ready for action, no one was concerned that only one person was in the center of everyone's gaze. Where was the man from last night? She did not even know his name.

She wanted to hide. Embarrassed, sick to her stomach, wondering if she would make it out of there alive, and if she did, how would she face her friends and family again? Where would she live? How would she make a living? Who would want to love her, much less marry her now—broken, it seemed, beyond repair. Could the shattered pieces of her life ever come together again to make something beautiful?

The men were demanding an answer from Jesus. Out of the corner of her eye, she saw He had knelt down and was writing something in the dirt. From her angle she could not quite make it out, but it appeared to be a list of some kind.

Their accusations were loud and chilling. There was no way to close them out. She shut her eyes tightly—hoping this day would end soon. Then she heard movement as Jesus rose to His feet.

She still could not look at Him. Everyone's voice faded, and the silence was deafening. The men were ready to hear what Jesus had to say, and everyone leaned in.

His voice was calm and gentle, yet there was a firmness to it. "Anyone of you who is without sin, you go ahead and be the one to throw the first stone!" And with that, He knelt back down to write some more. This time, He completed each line with something besides the list He had begun earlier.

She winced when the first stone hit the ground. Had they thrown it and missed? She was not quite sure. She listened, eyes clenched as she waited for the stone's impact. Was that noise a stone falling to the ground? There it was again and again. The sounds seemed to be moving further away than the first. She was too scared to look, but when it stopped, she lifted her head slightly to see what was coming next.

Just then, Jesus rose to His feet, wiping His hands. "Where did they go? Isn't anyone still here to condemn you for what you did?"

She was shocked and spoke quietly. "No one, Lord."

Jesus stepped closer, taking her hand in His, and with the other, He gently lifted her chin. Her focus slowly rose from the ground until He could finally see into her eyes. But what He really wanted was for her to gaze into His. With great compassion and unconditional love, He said, "Neither do I condemn you for what you have done. That is not who you are.

That is not who I made you to be." He paused as He wiped away a tear that ran down her face. "You are free to go. But, My child, do not live like that anymore. Change your ways. Follow Me and live like the precious woman I made you to be. Your sins are forgiven. You are loved deeply, and you matter to Me!"

Adapted from John 8:1–11

~ ~ ~ ~ ~

The Biblical Truth

There are wounded people all around us. You cannot live in this world affected by man's sin and not be touched by pain at one time or another. Some hide it well, finding clever ways to cover up the scars. Others drift through life with immense despondency and wonder: Is there any purpose in living when life seems to be falling apart? Can I trust in a God I cannot see— who does not seem to care? Can I believe or hope in anything? Does anyone love me, and does my life really matter?

Many of us have walked where they walk. We have felt hopelessness and despair. But we have found the answer in Jesus Christ. He loves us all and calls Christ-followers to show His love to others in distinct, observable ways.

Each day, we have opportunities to represent Christ to a world that desperately needs His touch. Life is wearisome at times. No matter if the cause of that heaviness is from personal decisions, choices that others made, or just plain challenging circumstances, the aching deep within seems to crush brokenhearted people. We can be Jesus' hands and feet to others, declaring to them how much they matter to God.

Jesus had a unique way of loving people. It was His nature to ignore and go against the grain of man's expectations for Him, taking a risk when it seemed the most unreasonable...all because He was living to serve and please His Father in heaven. He exposed sin and did not try to skirt around the facts. He spoke the truth about sin and did not always give people the answers they wanted to hear. His purpose was not for condemnation, but rather through loving them unconditionally, He revealed a better way.

> When we treasure Jesus with our heart, soul, and mind, it causes us to reflect His passionate love to others.

When we love like Jesus, it shows. It is not only profoundly evident to the person involved, but it is also widely visible to those who are watching. They wait to see how we will respond, how we will show that we care, and if we will follow through. When we treasure Jesus with our heart, soul, and mind, it causes us to reflect His passionate love to others. It might cost us, yet He is big enough to carry us through whatever we may face. Will we dare to trust Him, obeying what He asks of us? It is His kindness pouring out through us that will lead people to repentance.

Two pastors, a children's minister, and a couple of friends followed Jesus and modeled His love to me. They decided to put everything on the line to illustrate His tenderness toward me—continuing my employment after I had lied to them, giving of their time and resources as I lived with them, and helping me walk through strenuous times and work through complex questions. As they loved Jesus, His adoration spilled over to me, drawing me toward His heart to experience what they had. Their obedience to God echoed their affection for Him, and it reverberated in my life in a tremendous way.

~ ~ ~ ~ ~

Jesus' Love in Action

What does it look like to love others like Jesus? The exciting thing is it will be as diverse as God's creativity in each of us. We do not have to fit into a mold of loving others a certain way but can reflect God's love with variety as He places people and situations before us.

Jesus gave us some tangible examples in Scripture, such as loving intentionally, being available in uncomfortable situations, welcoming others to sit at His table, forgiving failures, risking vulnerability, and respecting people.[85] Let's review some of these encouraging scenes and join together in prayer, asking God to help us imitate that same kind of love.

Jesus Was Intentional

Jesus' love reached out to touch a leper—healing him both physically and emotionally.[86] There is an enormous healing power in someone's healthy touch. I experience this each time someone who knows my story reaches out to hold my hand in prayer. It warms my heart and reminds me that I am accepted, forgiven, and loved.

"Lord, open our eyes to see people around us who need Your healing touch. The AIDS patient, the depressed teen, the struggling single mom, the lonely college student, the fearful homeless person...each could use a gentle pat on the back, an affirming touch, or a helping hand for their overwhelming task. Teach us to be Your hands, touching people on purpose as You did, right where we are each day."

Jesus Was Available

Jesus' love risked being uncomfortable as He went into what was forbidden territory for a Jew at the time. Jesus and His disciples entered a graveyard to help a man who was hurting deeply, regardless of what was causing that pain, in order to bring him peace.[87]

"Lord, give us hearts to be available and a determination to help someone, even when it is uncomfortable. Help us not judge or question how they ended up in that position but show us ways to offer hope and the peace that You alone can bring."

Jesus Was Hospitable

Jesus ignored the looks, the whispers, and the scoffing of others in order to sit at a table, eating and fellowshipping with people who were despised in the community.[88] He risked putting His reputation on the line in order to love those who seemed unworthy to the crowd.

"Lord, we tend to protect our reputations, and our behavior is often propelled by what others will think and say about us. Forgive us for putting so much stake in their opinions. Help us to look past the exterior of people's lifestyle or their choices and see the need for You in their hearts and lives. Give us opportunities to welcome them into our homes to sit at our tables."

Jesus Was Forgiving

Jesus saw the potential in people and looked past their faults and failures in order to help them experience His extreme love.[89] He called together an unlikely team of disciples because He saw who they would become despite their flaws. He used them to spread His story of love and forgiveness.

"Lord, our views are so tainted by our opinions, the world's ideas of success, the church's belief of what is acceptable—each one may be valid in certain circumstances. But these can be so off-base from Your ideal. Give us eyes to see others as You see them. May we forgive quickly as we have been forgiven—realizing we are all broken. Help us remember that You made them and they are one of Your wonderful works—still a work in progress—just as we all are."

Jesus Was Vulnerable

Jesus did not worry about what others thought of Him as He received a questionable woman's loving gift of perfume that seemed unreasonable to onlookers.[90] He saw her heart, and receiving her love was worth more to Him than the approval of man.

> "Lord, give us opportunities to engage with people, and may we become so engrossed in talking with them that we forget about those around us who may be watching. Focus our hearts on communicating Your love to people, especially the marginalized—keeping their eternal destiny in mind."

Jesus Was Respectful

Jesus treated people with respect—those who otherwise did not fit in: the Samaritan woman, the children gathering around Him, those with illnesses... He stepped outside the box; the mission of loving sinners into the kingdom was more important to Jesus than anything else.[91]

People need to know and experience Jesus' unconditional compassion and that He wants to restore them to His original design for their lives.

"Lord, we confess we are often too busy to stop and consider how to love and respect. Slow us down enough to really see the needs and hurting hearts of those we, too easily, just walk right by. Help us be concerned for each soul we come in contact with."

As the body of Christ, we are here to love God, bring glory to His name, and love others as He has loved us.[92] People need to know and experience Jesus' unconditional compassion and that He wants to restore them to His original design for their lives. Our lifework and purpose is to guide others to see their true identity and need for Christ ("Therefore, go and make disciples...") walking the journey with them as they make decisions to follow ("...baptizing them...") and living close enough for them to see our relationship with God ("...teaching them to obey").[93]

~ ~ ~ ~ ~

Truth and the Twist

Truth

We are called to love God and to be a conduit of Jesus' unconditional love to others.

Twist on Truth

If I show love to the LGBTQ, I may be misunderstood as being gay; I may appear to be approving something that I really do not, or others may twist my words, saying I have ulterior motives; therefore,

    a. I will stay a safe distance away, and

    b. I will choose to not get involved, remaining as neutral as possible.

~ ~ ~ ~ ~

Untwisting Twisted Truth

One of Satan's greatest weapons is fear, which, to his advantage, effectively immobilizes the body of Christ. We fear saying the wrong thing and being labeled a bigot or homophobe. We fear declaring that the Word of God is the only truth. We fear befriending the LGBTQ and appearing as though we condone what they believe. Fear becomes magnified, and when it does, there is a natural tendency to withdraw and pull back from the front line. That is not loving people as Christ loved them.

God commands us to go, moving actively toward people, not away from them. It is necessary that we run to the battle and speak truth as we love them like Jesus. Fear stops us from moving forward to those who need His message of love, grace, and hope the most.

There is a portion of the great commission in Matthew 28:20 that recently stood out to me, "Teaching them to obey." Reflecting on this phrase, I asked, "Lord, how do I teach others to obey? I must first be walking in the way of obedience in order to be teaching someone else how to do the same. How can I tell others to obey You if they don't see me doing what You command? What if I choose not to follow You in obedience? What am I teaching then?"

The reality and weight of what I had just asked hit me like a ton of bricks. My choices and obedience, or lack thereof, directly impact others who are watching to gain insight as to how to take their next steps in their relationship with Christ. I continued in prayer.

"Father, I need to spend time in Your Word daily in order to learn the truths of Your precepts and know what to obey.

My life is to be essentially
a continual surrender to Him,
a continual release of my will,
to do His will—
a continual abandonment
to obedience
because others need to
see what that looks like in my life
as they learn to obey as well.

How will I know unless I study and seek out what You ask of me?" He gently reminded me that my life is to be essentially a continual surrender to Him, a continual release of my will, to do His will—a continual abandonment to obedience because others need to see what that looks like in my life as they learn to obey as well. I will not get it right every time, and I may have to apologize and ask for forgiveness, but they can also learn from my mistakes.

~ ~ ~ ~ ~

Community

How can we move closer, love others, and build relationships with the intention of drawing them to Jesus? Having been on the opposite side of the fence, I wondered how to connect with people who called themselves Christians. During a rather dark and lonely time in my life, I sat in a church and heard the pastor say, "We were made for community. You need to be in community. If you don't have this, you need to find some people to do life with." I agreed with him. I understood what he was talking about. But exactly how was I supposed to do that? The feelings of community and connectedness were somehow just out of my reach. My life was messy, and I did not seem to fit into any of the groups that were set up to promote community. I longed for fellowship with people where I could live life side by side, growing together.

Picture with me groups outside the church that seem to do community well: the brotherhood of first responders, biker groups, and the LGBTQ, to name a few. If Christ-followers want to have a community that draws others to the heart of Jesus, it will take work. Some people within church small groups really get it, while others are still wearing the masks and pretending.

What stops us in the body of Christ from experiencing this connectedness? Again, fear raises its ugly head. We fear others getting so close that they may see our scars, know where we have been, and realize who we truly are. We fear others might discover our shortfalls, think less of us, and judge us. We fear our mediocrity will stand out when compared to someone's excitement in following Jesus. We fear joining together with others because we don't know if we can jeopardize being real.

We must take the risk. We must be willing to allow God to expose our sin, to deal with it, and then invite someone close enough into our lives to teach them what obedience to a holy God looks like. But this cannot happen if we choose to hide our secret sins. Loving authentically also means living honestly as well. We cannot compromise or have double standards when it comes to our own struggles.

As we dare to love like Jesus in a world that does not understand His kind of love, stepping out of our own insecurities to make people feel welcome and accepted is critical, not just in our churches but in our daily lives as well. Can we risk sharing our lives in a way that would make others feel safe and comfortable? What if they do not believe like we do? What if they do not look like we do? What if they are not yet living a Christ-centered life? Are we okay with messy ministry?

In order to reach those who do not know Jesus or are not currently living a life of obedience, exhibiting a genuineness on our part first as we seek to build relationships is imperative.

When we are vulnerable, it allows others to also let down their guard. Broken people long for a place safe enough to open up about life's struggles, secure enough to love and be loved in a healthy manner, comfortable enough to be themselves— without condemnation—as we do life together and learn to follow Jesus.

This will cost us. It is difficult and scary to become real and transparent, but growth in our lives and those around us will not happen until we do. When we stop trying to impress and just reach out to love people, it will drastically change us. It is not about what they can do for us or what we can gain by being seen with them. Actually, the opposite is true. What might it cost us to be seen with that person? Will our reputations be tarnished? Can we afford an extra hour of our time? An extra night to meet to discuss their questions?

> It is difficult and scary to become real and transparent, but growth in our lives and those around us will not happen until we do.

Ministry with Jesus was messy. He did not have a three-phase plan, a catchy saying, a carefully laid out diagram detailing where to find people and how to connect them with other believers. He just lived...went about His Father's business... taught those around Him through daily life...loved people where they were...and challenged them, "Come and follow Me."

As shown earlier in the examples of Jesus loving people, we can start where He started: being intentional in our love, available whether it is convenient or not, hospitable as we welcome others to our table, forgiving because we are all broken people, vulnerable enough to share our pain and our story of how Jesus healed us, and respectful of those who are at a different spot in their journey. Our call is to be conduits of Jesus' love!

"Someone is waiting on the other side of your obedience!"[94]

Conclusion

> "He has sent me
> to bind up and heal the brokenhearted,
> "to proclaim liberty to the [physical and spiritual] captives
> "and the opening of the prison and
> of the eyes to those who are bound."[95]

Jesus came to redeem and restore each one of us so that we could have a relationship with Him. He is the only One who can heal our broken hearts, bring freedom, and open prison doors when we are chained in bondage. He did that for me, and He longs to do it for you too. I have nothing to offer you but Jesus and the hope that He brings. Any victory that has come to me is all because of Him. My life is not perfect, but I have learned to trust Him, even when life does not make sense. Although walking in this reality is a daily choice, I began to discover the validity of this fact at a young age.

"Jesus loves me, this I know, for the Bible tells me so."[96] I first sang that little song in early childhood, and the truth of those words became foundational to my worldview. Coming from a Christian home where we attended church every week,

I heard biblical theology in the old hymns and the truths of God's Word. My heart breaks for many today who do not have the same foundation. But regardless of where we come from, Satan works to lure us into the trap of believing his lies. Just the same, regardless of where we come from, God can expose the lies, draw us to Himself, and bring freedom.

Looking back over my story, I have contemplated more than once: if I was living in the homosexual lifestyle today and had an opportunity to walk away from it, would I? With all the propaganda and massive encouragement to follow my feelings with gay pride, would I have the strength and courage to leave the familiar and choose to follow Christ? In a society that is pushing us to accept the LGBTQ lifestyle as normal, I believe it would be much harder to come to the same conclusion today as I did many years ago. Although it must be an extremely difficult choice for anyone currently living among the confusion surrounding that mindset, believe me, it is worth every bit of the struggle to listen to God's gentle whisper and, by loving Jesus more, choose to follow Him. It is the only choice that will lead to living a life of true peace.

Despite the fact that it might be harder today, when God moves in the lives of people, anything is possible! It is imperative that we continue to pray daily that the Holy Spirit would melt the hearts of those who have exchanged the truth for a lie.[97] As Christ-followers, we cannot know God's truth and approve of continued LGBTQ behavior,[98] yet it is essential to be patient as those whom the Holy Spirit convicts work through the process of taking steps toward obedience to Christ. Renewal will come as truth is revealed through God's Word, which transforms our minds and false ideologies.[99]

~ ~ ~ ~ ~

Several years ago, I resigned from my children's ministry position and was wondering what God had for me next. While visiting a new church, I asked the pastor's wife how I could minister to her. She said she needed a friend—I could do that.

Little did I know God would bless me with a dear friend who soon became my coffee-drinking buddy. We spent so much time walking at the mall, the coffee shop staff told some people we knew, "These two blond ladies come so often; they really need to get a life!" So much laughter, a few tears, solving life's problems, and getting exercise all at the same time. We supported each other as we walked through both joy and pain. I had not experienced this kind of friendship since high school and was enjoying it immensely—until she told me they were moving away. I was thankful for the great opportunity they had been given, and at the same time, I was angry with God. I did not understand why He would take away another friend. I cried out to the Lord in my pain—and He answered.

"Lord, why are You taking her away? It feels like such a deep wound to lose another friend. Why do I feel like this? Is this normal? Why would You give me a healthy friendship and then take it away? Did I do something wrong? Do I feel something that's not pleasing to You?"

"Marilyn, this is not about you. Her family is moving because of the next steps I have planned in their lives. I gave you her friendship as a gift to know what it is like to have a really good friend who is female. You needed to know that it is okay to love deeply and have girlfriends. I made you for community, to love others like I love you and express that love in a healthy way.

You were made new to love and live abundantly! Now, show the world My love through your life!"

For years, I had kept all males at arm's length because I did not think they were safe. Following additional pain, I began to do the same with females because of the sexual abuse I had experienced. I did not feel safe with people, so I made sure to not allow anyone too close into my life. In time, God brought healing regarding my fear of males, and to my amazement, I was married. Then, He gave me a female friend and told me it was good. That was nearly thirteen years after I had left the homosexual lifestyle, and I had no idea there were still wounded places that God was working on. He gave me the gift of a friend and healed me where I did not even know I had a need. That is my Savior's heart!

> He gave me the gift of a friend and healed me where I did not even know I had a need. That is my Savior's heart!

There is such confusion for today's children, teens, and young adults during this time when being gay, having a fluid identity, or becoming transgender becomes more of a trend. Some kids wonder if they are gay just because they have close friendships with the same sex. As a young adult, I was confused and did not know what a normal friendship was or if I could have close female friends. Because of the disorientation many people are facing, there is an enormous mission field to reach these young people right in our backyard. It is imperative that we speak truth into their lives as they struggle to work through the maze of perplexity regarding identity.

~ ~ ~ ~ ~

Body of Christ

As the body of Christ, we have an opportunity to assist in setting captives free—both physically and spiritually. Physically, there may be situations where we might need to take someone into our home or offer to assist in their housing and physical needs as they choose to walk away from a partner. Emotions run high within domestic situations, and LGBTQ relationships are no different. While we need to exercise wisdom and discernment, we also have the privilege of walking alongside new believers and those returning to the Lord as they take new steps of obedience. Our example comes from Jesus, as He spent time with people, getting to know them, listening to their stories, yet standing firm in God's ways and calling them to truth.

Setting captives free spiritually will include open conversations that may be uncomfortable at times. It will also encompass a depth of mentoring that may seem rather monumental. Someone coming out of that lifestyle has believed an assortment of lies and will need gentleness as we love them and assist in their discipleship. As we get to know those who are struggling, we must offer them true community with Christ at the center, showing them what godly friendships look like. They have, no doubt, experienced community with their LGBTQ friends, but there is nothing like having community with Jesus as the center of our relationships. Be patient with them as they seek to find their place. It is uncomfortable. It is scary. It takes a lot of effort, and they may not get it right all the time. Give them room to make mistakes—just like we would with anyone learning to walk with Jesus. Give them freedom to ask hard questions without judgment. Remember Jesus delights in our baby steps!

~ ~ ~ ~ ~

Parents

Parents, wherever you find yourself today, remember that Jesus is right there with you. If you are struggling with your child's choices and how to communicate without a fight—if you are wondering how to love this person that now identifies as a different gender than from what you gave birth to, if you are wrestling with meeting the new same-sex partner...Jesus knows your distress. He understands your confusion. He can handle your anger. He hears your cries for help, and He promises to never leave you. Are you brokenhearted? Yes—but He came to bind up your brokenness. Seek to rest in His arms and cling to His unfailing love. He will guide your steps and give you the words to say. God is still in control. He sees you and is walking with you through this trial.

Regardless of what Satan will tell you, know that you are not to blame. We raise our kids to the best of our ability, doing many things right and making a few mistakes along the way. We can come before our loving God to confess our shortfalls, learn from the mistakes, and move on. The bottom line is—our kids have a free will to make their own choices in life, and one of the hardest things we have to do as parents is stand back and let them. Sometimes we know their decisions will bring them trouble and heartache. Sometimes we can help, but many times, they just need us to be there for them when life does not turn out as they had planned.

During a painfully difficult time while raising my boys, I was told something that was hard to hear but nevertheless very wise, "God is writing their life story too!" What? I wanted to write their story. I wanted a say in how their life would go. I wanted to make everything work out well for them and protect them from emotional and physical suffering. But each decision, each hurt, each difficulty they face is an opportunity to grow stronger and to ultimately learn to lean on the Lord.

I encourage you to stand strong in your faith and be unwavering in your commitment to the truth of God's Word. He is still on the throne. His Word is unchanging, and the principles set forth in His Word have not changed. Although our culture would like us to adjust and accept changing standards, we must stay committed to God's plumb line of truth.

Pray! Pray! And pray some more! God is faithful and loves your child more than you do. Release your child to Him. Trust Him to do His work in His timing, in His way!

~ ~ ~ ~ ~

LGBTQ

To the LGBTQ, you are loved, and you matter to Jesus, to me, and to many others! There are people who love Jesus and

> ### Jesus does not want to fight you but love you and embrace your wounded heart.

want to love you like He does. There are people who will listen to your story and not judge you. They cannot compromise on God's truth, but they understand that we are all sinners and growing in our journey toward Jesus.

I encourage you to surrender the battle. You know the fight I am talking about: the constant unrest, defending yourself, questioning decisions, wondering where you stand...Satan is trying to twist things up in your mind—making life harder than it really needs to be. Jesus does not want to fight you but love you and embrace your wounded heart.

God is okay with baby steps. Whatever you can entrust to Him at this point—whatever you can surrender to His love...He is okay with it taking some time. He knows you will not get it right every time, and that is okay. He is crazy about you and wants to be your very best friend! Take one step. Just do what God tells you to do through His Word, the Bible. Give it a try. Take the risk. You will

> ### Jesus wants to free you from the prisons and bondage you do not even know you are in.

lose some friends, but you will gain deeper friendships, a peace beyond your understanding, and eternity in heaven. It will be worth it in the end, trust me. Jesus wants to free you from the prisons and bondage you do not even know you are in.

If you have tried reaching out to a Christ-follower and it did not go well, I am sorry. Whatever someone said that discouraged you as you tried to learn about Jesus, I am sorry. Whatever their look said to you as you tried to visit a church, I am sorry. Sometimes people say things that are just plain ugly. Press through that! Know that if you try to take any step, even those baby steps toward Jesus, Satan will be working overtime to try to keep you away. Press through! Just like the woman in the Bible who had to risk condemnation to press through and touch the hem of Jesus' garment to be healed,[100] do it. Press through the crowd! Press through and do not stop until you reach Jesus. His love is unfailing and is not meant to harm you. There may be some other wounded people who might bruise you along the way. They are hurting in their own way. Press on past them! Just get to Jesus any way you can. You will not be sorry.

> Just get to Jesus any way you can. You will not be sorry.

I love you! You are always welcome at my table!

~ ~ ~ ~ ~

Yes, Jesus loves [you]
Yes, Jesus loves [you]
Yes, Jesus loves [you]
The Bible tells you so![101]

The Rest of the Story... Forgiveness

The Rest of the Story—Jack

God brought Jack's forgiveness full circle...

Twelve years after God asked me to forgive Jack, I ran into him again. By this time, he was married and had children of his own. He had tried to find me a couple of times through the years but was unsuccessful. After a little small talk, through tear-filled eyes, he asked, "Will you forgive me?"

Forgiveness is truly a beautiful, freeing thing because I had no anger whatsoever toward him. However, I was a little confused. "Jack, I forgave you years ago."

"I know, but I've got to hear you say it. Will you please forgive me?"

"Yes, indeed! I forgive you!"

The weight was lifted, and there was true freedom for both of us!

Reference chapter 5

~ ~ ~ ~ ~

The Rest of the Story—Pastor Jonathan

The freedom that comes with being forgiven is amazing.

As I wrote about meeting with my pastors, I was again overwhelmed by the way Pastor Jonathan handled my situation and the grace that was poured out. Contacting him in the midst of this writing, I asked, "How did you know to do that? Back in the 80s, how did you know to deal with me the way you did?"

His gentleness was still evident. "I acted out of a desire to minister and wanted to love you like Jesus."

His encouragement to complete this project helped me press on numerous times!

Reference chapter 9

~ ~ ~ ~ ~

The Rest of the Story—Kris

Forgiveness without actually speaking to the person and telling them still works.

The last time I spoke to Kris was after my trip to Deaf Camp in 1987 when God told me to cut things off completely. She knew my prayer was for her to return to the Lord. What that looked like and when or if that would take place was out of my control. She knew I did not want retaliation for what she had done but desired for her restoration with the Lord.

I do not know exactly when I forgave Kris, but as I prayed for her those early years after leaving, I released her to the Lord for Him to deal with as He saw fit. Freedom for me came as I moved on with life—totally forgiving and forgiven!

Reference chapter 13

~ ~ ~ ~ ~

The Rest of the Story—My Parents and Siblings

Upon returning home to reconcile with my family, there was one sibling I was unable to see during that Christmas visit. Her family lived too far away to include in the "Forgiveness Tour"; however, we were able to connect at a later date, and it was as sweet as the reunions had been with the other siblings.

I continued to have a good relationship with my parents, whose faith has become sight since they entered heaven. My siblings and I communicate often, although we don't get together much because we are still spread out all over the United States. They are precious to me, and their gift of forgiveness is priceless!

Reference chapter 13

~ ~ ~ ~ ~

The Rest of the Story—My Previous Marriage

Four years after I walked away from my lesbian relationship, I met a man at the church where I was serving in children's ministry. One week after our first date, I told him my story of God's grace in my life, and the next day, I shared it with his parents. At that time, they strongly advised me that I was to never speak of this again. I had no desire to put it in the bulletin or on the church sign, so I agreed. Although there were some red flags I chose to ignore, we were married after a short time of dating and engagement.

We spent seventeen years married, followed by three years in a divorce battle. Although straight, his moral path became crooked at that time as his life appeared to drift further from the Lord. I was given my greatest compliment from him as he said, "You did all that Jesus stuff when we were first married—but over the years, you got worse!"

The battle is not against flesh and blood but against rulers and principalities of the air. From my perspective, Satan stepped in and twisted the truth for my husband. He was not the same man I married. Something had changed. This has been my greatest challenge in forgiveness, but I continually work to give him over to the Lord.

~ ~ ~ ~ ~

The Rest of the Story—My Children

I am now free to share my testimony in order to show others that choosing Jesus and a life of obedience to Him is not only possible but absolutely worth it. I have my children's full blessing to share all God has done. In fact, when I asked them what they thought of me writing a book, they wondered what took me so long to begin. We continue to experience God's faithfulness and are convinced that He can be trusted, even when life doesn't make sense!

My Identity in Christ

"SEARCH MY HEART, O GOD"	"LEAD ME IN TRUTH"	"GOD'S WORD IS TRUTH"
Labels/Adjectives I Wear	Who Jesus Sees I Am	Scripture Support
1.	1.	1.
2.	2.	2.
3.	3.	3.
4.	4.	4.
5.	5.	5.
6.	6.	6.
7.	7.	7.
8.	8.	8.
9.	9.	9.
10.	10.	10.
11.	11.	11.
12.	12.	12.
13.	13.	13.
14.	14.	14.

Reference chapter 19

Resources

Barr, Adam T., and Ron Citlau. *Compassion without Compromise: How the Gospel Frees Us to Love Our Gay Friends without Losing the Truth*. Bethany House Publishers, 2014.

Brown, Michael L., PhD. *Can You Be Gay and Christian? Responding with Love and Truth to Questions about Homosexuality*. FrontLine, 2014.

Christenson, Evelyn. *Lord, Change Me!* Evelyn Christenson Ministry, 2008.

Dallas, Joe. *When Homosexuality Hits Home: What to Do When a Family Member Says They're Gay*. Reprint, Harvest House Publishers, 2015.

Howard, Jeanette. *Out of Egypt*. Monarch Publishing, 1991.

Hubbard, Peter. *Love into Light: The Gospel, the Homosexual and the Church*. Emerald House Group, 2013.

Johnson, Barbara. *Where Does a Mother Go to Resign?* Bethany House Publishers, 1994.

McDowell, Josh, and Sean McDowell. *Evidence That Demands a Verdict: Life-Changing Truth for a Skeptical World*. Thomas Nelson, 2017.

Paulk, Anne. *Restoring Sexual Identity: Hope for Women Who Struggle with Same-Sex Attraction.* Harvest House Publishers, 2003.

Restored Hope Network. www.restoredhopenetwork.org.

Seiler, Linda, Dr. *Compassion Without Compromise: A Christian Response to Homosexuality.* https://lindas-courses.thinkific.com/courses/compassion-without-compromise.

Strobel, Lee. *The Case for Christ: A Journalist's Personal Investigation of the Evidence for Jesus.* Zondervan, 2016.

Statement of Faith

The Bible

I believe the Bible is the very Word of God, inspired by the Holy Spirit, written through man to communicate His great love and truth to the world. It is completely without error, unchangeable, trustworthy, and the final authority for life.

One God

I believe there is one God who is loving, holy, infinite, and all-powerful. He exists eternally in three persons: God the Father, God the Son, and God the Holy Spirit—each possessing equal attributes of Deity.

Jesus Christ

I believe Jesus Christ became man without ceasing to be God and was conceived by the Holy Spirit and born of a virgin so that He might reveal God and redeem a sinful mankind. Through His sinless life and voluntary death on the cross as a substitution sacrifice, He accomplished our redemption, which is made sure by His literal bodily resurrection from the dead. He is now in heaven, seated at the right hand of God, as our High Priest.

Holy Spirit

I believe in the personal involvement of the Holy Spirit, who convicts and draws sinners to Christ, imparts new life, continually lives within, and guides Christians from the moment of spiritual birth, enabling them to live a godly life.

Man

I believe God created man, male and female, in His image with a free will to choose obedience or to reject His ways. In Adam's rebellion the human race fell, inherited a sinful nature, became alienated from God, and can be restored to God's favor only through the work of Jesus Christ. In order to receive that salvation, man must repent of his sin and place his trust in Jesus Christ alone for salvation.

Salvation

I believe Jesus Christ is the only way to salvation, not by any human efforts. Salvation is a free gift of God received by grace through personal faith in the Lord Jesus Christ, whose blood was shed for the forgiveness of our sins.

Eternity

I believe all people will live eternally: believers in the state of conscious fellowship with the Lord and eternal life and unbelievers in the state of conscious separation from the Lord and eternal punishment.

Sanctity of Human Life

I believe God creates all human beings in His image, designing our DNA and gender from the point of conception. All human life is sacred and should be protected from its beginning and conception to its natural end.

Human Sexuality

I believe God's design for human sexuality is to be expressed exclusively within the union of a monogamous marriage of one biological male and one biological female. This marriage blueprint was instituted by God as the foundation of the family and the basic structure of human society.

About the Author

Marilyn has circled America several times, having had the opportunity to live in five states. She loves to travel, take road trips, and explore places off the beaten path with her two sons. Although they often say she's lost, she maintains they are merely "creatively exploring."

Following her prodigal journey, Marilyn was married for seventeen years before moving to Virginia with her boys. She raised her sons as a single mom and continued to homeschool. As the boys graduated, she began to pursue her next calling—to share her story of how God can change a life that is surrendered and devoted to Him.

Through life's ups and downs, Marilyn has held to her faith in a loving God whose character we can trust, even when nothing else makes sense. She's learned to keep her focus on and faith in God even when people bring pain and abuse. Abba has been and continues to be her Provider, Protector, Deliverer, Defender, Rock, Refuge, Sustainer, Savior, Lord, and Best Friend! To Him alone be all the glory!

Contact Information

Website: *www.HealedHeart.net*
Email: *Marilyn@HealedHeart.net.*

Notes

1. "Rise Again," track on Dallas Holm, *Dallas Holm and Praise Live*, Going Holm Music Publishers, 1977.
2. Matthew 18:21–22 (NIV).
3. Psalm 37:23 (NKJV).
4. www.dictionary.com.
5. "It Is Finished," track 12 on William J. and Gloria Gaither, *Classic Moments from The Bill Gaither Trio, Vol. 1*, Hanna Street Music (BMI), 1976.
6. Ibid.
7. Ibid.
8. "The Artist," track 6 on Buck & Dottie Rambo, Reaching Around the World, Songs of Rambo McGuire/SESAC, 1986.
9. Ibid.
10. John 8:1–11.
11. See Romans 4:17–21.
12. "Runner," track 1 on Twila Paris, *Kingdom Seekers*, Mountain Spring Music (ASCAP) Straightway Music (ASCAP), 1985.
13. "Do I Trust You," track 4 on Twila Paris, *Warrior Is a Child*, New Spring Publishing Inc. (ASCAP), 1984.
14. "Every Heart That Is Breaking," track 2 on Twila Paris, *For Every Heart*, Mountain Spring Music (ASCAP) Ariose Music (ASCAP), 1988.
15. "Sweet Victory," track 1 on Twila Paris, *For Every Heart*,

Mountain Spring Music (ASCAP) Ariose Music (ASCAP), 1988.

16 "The Refiner's Fire," track 5 on Steve Green. *The Mission*, Birdwing Music/Jonathan Mark Music/J.R. Dennis Music, 1989.

17 Jeremiah 33:3 (NIV).

18 www.webstersdictionary1828.com.

19 www.websters1913.com.

20 www.wordcentral.com.

21 www.learnersdictionary.com.

22 www.yourdictionary.com.

23 www.time.com (November 15, 2016).

24 "Truth," Bible Study Tools, accessed January 30, 2018, https://www.biblestudytools.com/dictionaries/bakers-evan-gelical-dictionary/truth.html.

25 Ibid (see Romans 1:18, Romans 1:25).

26 Hebrews 13:8 (NIV).

27 www.dictionary.com.

28 See appendix C. Further reading: Josh McDowell and Lee Stroble.

29 Titus 1:2.

30 www.dictionary.com.

31 Romans 5:12–21.

32 Romans 3:10 (NIV).

33 Romans 3:23 (NIV).

34 Romans 6:23 (NIV).

35 Ibid.

36 Psalm 37:23 (AMPC).

37 1 John 2:1.

38 1 John 1:6–8 (NIV).

39 1 John 4:9 (NIV).

40 John 3:16 (NIV). Blanks and adaptation added by author to personalize text.

41 Ibid.

42 John 3:16 (AMPC).

43 John 3:16. Blanks and adaptation added by author to per-

sonalize text.

44 www.dictionary.com

45 "John 3," Bible Study Tools, https://www.biblestudytools.com/commentaries/scofield-reference-notes/john/john-3.html.

46 John 3:16. Blanks and adaptation added by author to personalize text.

47 John 3:17 (NIV).

48 Romans 5:8 (NIV).

49 1 John 3:16 (NIV).

50 1 John 4:10 (NIV).

51 1 John 4:18 (NIV).

52 Psalm 32:10 (NIV). "Person" used for "man."

53 Psalm 103:8 (NIV).

54 1 John 5:3 (NIV).

55 2 John 1:6 (NIV).

56 Romans 6:23 (NIV).

57 1 John 5:3 (NIV).

58 1 John 1:9.

59 Psalm 51:7.

60 Revelation 3:20 (NIV). [Of your heart] added by author for clarification.

61 1 John 1:9 (NIV).

62 1 John 1:10 (NIV).

63 1 John 1:5–6 (NIV).

64 Matthew 19:26.

65 Hebrews 13:5 (NIV).

66 Luke 15:10 (NIV).

67 John 14:6.

68 John 8:32.

69 Matthew 16:13–20.

70 John 4:1–26.

71 2 Corinthians 6:18.

72 Unknown quote.

73 www.dictionary.com.

74 1 Peter 1:15–16.

75 See appendix B: My Identity In Christ.

76 Philippians 1:6 (AMP).

77 1 Peter 5:8 (NIV).

78 Various YouTube videos:

"Dramatic Lion Action: Lion Stalk and Catch Buffalo Cow & Newborn Calf!" video, 10:58, https://www.youtube.com/watch?v=GQa-v7Hzcdc.

"The Life of the King of the African Jungle—Lion Documentary HD," video, 43:56, https://youtu.be/CUm1A-pFuR4.

"Lions on the Prowl: Nature Documentary on the Large African Predators," video, 1:18:44, https://www.youtube.com/watch?v=BUQMHERmKes.

"Lions vs. Zebra | World's Deadliest," accessed May 17, 2018, video, 3:04, https://www.youtube.com/watch?v=KGRebpx03RE.

"Lions vs. Hyenas: Predator Games Killer IQ: Full Episode | Smithsonian Channel," video, 46:08, https://youtu.be/s2VpqlxlB5s.

79 Colossians 2:8 (NIV).

80 Ephesians 6:11–13 (AMP).

81 Ephesians 6:10 (AMP).

82 "John Bradford," Quotes, https://www.quotes.net/authors/John+Bradford.

83 Combination of personal thoughts and ideas from www.fromtheheartart.com, www.biblestudytools.com/commentaries/matthew-henry-complete/ephesians/, and The Amplified Bible.

84 James 4:7 (NIV).

85 Justin Deeter, "6 Ways You Can Create Authentic Community in Your Church," last modified November 3, 2014, https://www.justindeeter.com/articles/archives/2108.

86 Luke 5:12–14 (Jesus heals a leper).

87 Mark 5:1–20 (Jesus heals demon-possessed man in graveyard).

88 Luke 5:29–31 (Jesus has fellowship with despised people, tax collectors, and sinners).

89 Mark 1:16–20, Matthew 16:18 (Jesus calls disciples/Jesus calls Peter the rock).
90 Luke 7:36–50 (Jesus receives sinful woman's gift of oil).
91 John 4:1–26 (Jesus speaks to the Samaritan woman).
92 Matthew 22:37–39.
93 Matthew 28:19–20 (NIV).
94 Dr. David Uth, Sunday Sermon, First Baptist Church, Orlando, 2010.
95 Isaiah 61:1 (AMPC).
96 Anna Bartlett Warner, "Jesus Loves Me, This I Know," 1859.
97 Romans 1:25.
98 Romans 1:32.
99 Romans 12:2.
100 Matthew 9:18–22.
101 Bartlett Warner, "Jesus Loves Me, This I Know."